teacher's friend publications

MAY

a creative idea book
for the
elementary teacher

written and illustrated
by
Karen Sevaly

edited by
Shelley Price

Reproduction of these materials for commercial resale or distribution to an entire school or school district is strictly prohibited. Pages may be duplicated for one individual classroom set only. Material may not be reproduced for other purposes without the prior written permission of the publisher.

Copyright © 1988, 1997
Teacher's Friend Publications, Inc.
All rights reserved.
Printed in the United States of America
Published by Teacher's Friend Publications, Inc.
3240 Trade Center Dr., Riverside, CA 92507

ISBN-0-943263-08-5

This book is dedicated
to teachers and children
everywhere.

Table of Contents

MAKING THE MOST OF IT! 7
    What Is in This Book 8
    How to Use This Book 8
    Adding the Color 9
    Lamination 9
    Photocopies and Ditto Masters 10
    Monthly Organizers 11
    Bulletin Board Ideas 11
    Lettering and Headings 12

CALENDAR - MAY! 13
    May Calendar and Activities 14
    May Calendar Header 17
    May Calendar Symbols 18
    May - Blank Calendar 20

MAY ACTIVITIES! 21
    May Bookmarks 22
    May Awards 23
    May Pencil Toppers 24
    Flower Paper Bag Puppet 25
    Flower Patterns 26
    May Booklet Cover 27
    Certificate of Recognition 28
    Student of the Month Certificate 29
    Field Trip Ideas! 30
    We're Going on a Field Trip! Page 32
    My Field Trip Record 33
    Field Trip Visor 34

MAY DAY! 35
    May Day - May 1st 36
    May Basket 37
    International Children - Russia 38
    Mini Flower Booklets 40
    My Flower Report 42
    Matching Flower Pots 43
    Plants and Flowers! 44
    Parts of a Flower 46
    Plant Markers and Green Thumb Award 47
    Growing Flower Craft 48
    My Garden Book 49
    Repeat Patterns 54

MOTHER'S DAY! ...55

- Mother's Day - 2nd Sunday in May ...56
- Happy Mother's Day Certificate ...57
- My Special Mother's Day Pledge! ...58
- Mother's Day Crafts! ...59
- Mother's Day Basket ...61
- 3-D Flower Card ...62
- Mother's Day Rose ...63
- My Mom is Special! Pages ...64
- Mother's Day Creative Writing ...66

CINCO DE MAYO! ...67

- Cinco de Mayo - May 5th! ...68
- Flag of Mexico ...69
- Ojo de Dios! ...70
- Cinco de Mayo Finger Puppets ...71
- The Ancient People of Mexico! ...72
- Maya Pyramid Staircase ...74
- Aztec Calendar ...75
- Mexican Food! ...76
- Spanish Bingo Words ...76
- Spanish Bingo Card ...77
- Mexican Hat Dance ...78

OUR FEATHERED FRIENDS! ...79

- Bird Watching Activities! ...80
- Bird Feeders! ...82
- Bird Paper Bag Puppet ...84
- Duck Tales ...86
- Flying Birds Mobile ...87
- Mother Bird Game Board ...88
- Parts of a Bird ...90
- My Bird Watching Book! ...91
- Duckling Pattern! ...99
- Bird Names Word Find ...99
- Bird Sequence Cards ...100

THE BIG TOP! ...101

- Circus Activities! ...102
- Circus Finger Puppets ...104
- Movable Clown ...105
- Three-Ring Circus ...106
- Elephant Paper Bag Puppet ...108
- Elephant Mask ...110
- Circus Word Find! ...112

Stand-Up Circus Animals 113
Create a Clown Face! 114
Clown Wheel 116
Mr. Clown 118
My Circus Report 119
Clown Color Page 120
My Circus Book 121
Circus Writing Page 122

ZOO ANIMALS! 123

Zoo Animal Activities! 124
My Zoo Animal Report 127
Hippo Paper Bag Puppet 128
Lion Paper Bag Puppet 129
Lion Paper Topper 130
Stand-Up Zoo Animals 132
Hippo Patterns 134

BULLETIN BOARDS AND MORE! 135

Bulletin Boards and More! 136
Bird Patterns 139
Hanging Monkey 140
Giraffe Pattern 141
Elephant Sign 142
Clown Sign 143

ANSWER KEY! 144

Making the most of it!

WHAT IS IN THIS BOOK:

You will find the following in each monthly idea book from Teacher's Friend Publications:

1. A calendar listing every day of the month with a classroom idea and mention of special holidays and events.

2. At least four student awards to be sent home to parents.

3. Three or more bookmarks that can be used in your school library or given to students by you as "Super Student Awards."

4. Numerous bulletin board ideas and patterns pertaining to the particular month and seasonal activity.

5. Easy-to-make craft ideas related to the monthly holidays and special days.

6. Dozens of activities emphasizing not only the obvious holidays, but also the often forgotten celebrations such as May Day and Cinco de Mayo.

7. Creative writing pages, crossword puzzles, word finds, booklet covers, games, paper bag puppets, literature lists and much more!

8. Scores of classroom management techniques and methods proven to motivate your students to improve behavior and classroom work.

HOW TO USE THIS BOOK:

Every page of this book may be duplicated for individual classroom use.

Some pages are meant to be copied or used as duplicating masters. Other pages may be transferred onto construction paper or used as they are.

If you have access to a print shop, you will find that many pages work well when printed on index paper. This type of paper takes crayons and felt markers well and is sturdy enough to last. (Bookmarks work particularly well on index paper.)

Lastly, some pages are meant to be enlarged with an overhead or opaque projector. When we say enlarge, we mean it! Think BIG! Three, four or even five feet is great! Try using colored butcher paper or poster board so you don't spend all your time coloring.

ADDING THE COLOR:

Putting the color to finished items can be a real bother to teachers in a rush. Try these ideas:

1. On small areas, watercolor markers work great. If your area is rather large, switch to crayons or even colored chalk or pastels.

   (Don't worry, lamination or a spray fixative will keep color on the work and off of you. No laminator or fixative? That's okay, a little hair spray will do the trick.)

2. The quickest method of coloring large items is to start with colored paper. (Poster board, butcher paper or large construction paper work well.) Add a few dashes of a contrasting colored marker or crayon and you will have it made.

3. Try cutting character eyes, teeth, etc. from white typing paper and gluing them in place. These features will really stand out and make your bulletin boards come alive.

   For special effects, add real buttons or lace. Metallic paper looks great on stars and belt buckles, too.

LAMINATION:

If you have access to a roll laminator, then you already know how fortunate you are. They are priceless when it comes to saving time and money. Try these ideas:

1. You can laminate more than just classroom posters and construction paper. Try various kinds of fabric, wallpaper and gift wrapping. You'll be surprised at the great combinations you come up with.

   Laminated classified ads can be used to cut headings for current events bulletin boards. Colorful gingham fabric makes terrific cut letters or bulletin board trim. You might even try burlap! Bright foil gift wrapping paper will add a festive feeling to any bulletin board.

   (You can even make professional looking bookmarks with laminated fabric or burlap. They are great holiday gift ideas for Mom or Dad!)

2. Felt markers and laminated paper or fabric can work as a team. Just make sure the markers you use are permanent and not water-based. Oops, make a mistake! That's okay. Put a little ditto fluid on a tissue, rub across the mark and presto, it's gone! Also, dry transfer markers work great on lamination and can easily be wiped off.

Teacher's Friend Publications, Inc. ©   TF0500 May Idea Book

LAMINATION:
(continued)

3. Laminating cut-out characters can be tricky. If you have enlarged an illustration onto poster board, simply laminate first and then cut it out with scissors or an art knife. (Just make sure the laminator is hot enough to create a good seal.)

   One problem may arise when you paste an illustration onto poster board and laminate the finished product. If your paste-up is not 100% complete, your illustration and posterboard may separate after laminating. To avoid this problem, paste your illustration onto poster board that measures slightly larger than the illustration. This way, the lamination will help hold down your paste-up.

4. When pasting up your illustration, always try to use either rubber cement, artist's spray adhesive or a glue stick. White glue, tape or paste does not laminate well because it can often be seen under your artwork.

5. Have you ever laminated student-made place mats, crayon shavings, tissue paper collages, or dried flowers? You'll be amazed at the variety of creative things that can be laminated and used in the classroom or as take-home gifts.

PHOTOCOPIES AND DITTO MASTERS:

Many of the pages in this book can be copied for use in the classroom. Try some of these ideas for best results:

1. If the print from the back side of your original comes through the front when making a photocopy or ditto master, slip a sheet of black construction paper behind the sheet. This will mask the unwanted shadows and create a much better copy.

2. Several potential masters in this book contain instructions for the teacher. Simply cover the type with correction fluid or a small slip of paper before duplicating.

3. When using a new ditto master, turn down the pressure on the duplicating machine. As the copies become light, increase the pressure. This will get longer wear out of both the master and the machine.

4. Trying to squeeze one more run out of that worn ditto master can be frustrating. Try lightly spraying the inked side of the master with hair spray. For some reason, this helps the master put out those few extra copies.

MONTHLY ORGANIZERS:

Staying organized month after month, year after year can be a real challenge. Try this simple idea:

After using the loose pages from this book, file them in their own file folder labeled with the month's name. This will also provide a place to save pages from other reproducible books along with craft ideas, recipes and articles you find in magazines and periodicals. (*Essential Pocket Folders* by Teacher's Friend provide a perfect way to store your monthly ideas and reproducibles. Each *Monthly Essential Pocket Folder* comes with a sixteen-page booklet of essential patterns and organizational ideas. There are even special folders for *Back to School*, *The Substitute Teacher* and *Parent-Teacher Conferences*.)

You might also like to dedicate a file box for every month of the school year. A covered box will provide room to store large patterns, sample art projects, certificates and awards, monthly stickers, monthly idea books and much more.

BULLETIN BOARDS IDEAS:

Creating clever bulletin boards for your classroom need not take fantastic amounts of time and money. With a little preparation and know-how, you can have different boards each month with very little effort. Try some of these ideas:

1. Background paper should be put up only once a year. Choose colors that can go with many themes and holidays. The black butcher paper background you used as a spooky display in October will have a special dramatic effect in April with student-made, paper-cut butterflies.

2. Butcher paper is not the only thing that can be used to cover the back of your board. You might also try fabric from a colorful bed sheet or gingham material. Just fold it up at the end of the year to reuse again. Wallpaper is another great background cover. Discontinued rolls can be purchased for a small amount at discount hardware stores. Most can be wiped clean and will not fade like construction paper. (Do not glue wallpaper directly to the board; just staple or pin in place.)

3. Store your bulletin board pieces in large, flat envelopes made from two large sheets of tagboard or cardboard. Simply staple three sides together and slip the pieces inside. (Small pieces can be stored in zip-lock, plastic bags.) Label your large envelopes with the name of the bulletin board and the month and year you displayed it. Take a picture of each bulletin board display. Staple the picture to your storage envelope. Next year when you want to create the same display, you will know right where everything goes. Kids can even follow your directions when you give them a picture to look at.

Teacher's Friend Publications, Inc. ©   TF0500 May Idea Book

LETTERING AND HEADINGS:

Not every school has a letter machine that produces perfect 4" letters. The rest of us will just have to use the old stencil-and-scissor method. But wait, there is an easier way!

1. Don't cut individual letters as they are difficult to pin up straight, anyway. Instead, hand print bulletin board titles and headings onto strips of colored paper. When it is time for the board to come down, simply roll it up to use again next year. If you buy your own pre-cut lettering, save yourself some time and hassle by pasting the desired statements onto long strips of colored paper. Laminate if possible. These can be rolled up and stored the same way!

   Use your imagination! Try cloud shapes and cartoon bubbles. They will all look great.

2. Hand lettering is not that difficult, even if your printing is not up to penmanship standards. Print block letters with a felt marker. Draw big dots at the end of each letter. This will hide any mistakes and add a charming touch to the overall effect.

   If you are still afraid to freehand it, try this nifty idea: Cut a strip of poster board about 28" X 6". Down the center of the strip, cut a window with an art knife measuring 20" X 2". There you have it: a perfect stencil for any lettering job. All you need to do is write capital letters with a felt marker within the window slot. Don't worry about uniformity. Just fill up the entire window height with your letters. Move your poster-board strip along as you go. The letters will always remain straight and even because the poster board window is straight.

3. If you must cut individual letters, use construction paper squares measuring 4 1/2" X 6". (Laminate first if you can.) Cut the capital letters as shown. No need to measure; irregular letters will look creative and not messy.

Calendar

May!

Teacher's Friend Publications, Inc. ©   13   TF0500 May Idea Book

1ˢᵀ   Today is MAY DAY! (Have your students surprise someone with a spring bouquet of flowers or have your class perform a May dance around the school flagpole.)

2ᴺᴰ   Celebrate BACKWARDS DAY! (Leonardo da Vinci was a master at writing backwards. Ask your students to try their hand at it. Provide a mirror to help decipher their messages.

3ᴿᴰ   Today marks the first observance of SUN DAY. (Hold a class discussion about solar energy.)

4ᵀᴴ   HORACE MANN, considered the father of free public education, was born on this day in 1796. (Discuss the advantages of a free education with your students.)

5ᵀᴴ   On this day, Mexico celebrates CINCO DE MAYO in commemoration of the victory at the battle of Puebla, in 1862. (Break a piñata in celebration of this festive occasion.)

6ᵀᴴ   Today is NATIONAL NURSES' DAY! (Ask your students to write a special thank you note to your school nurse.)

7ᵀᴴ   Composers JOHANNES BRAHMS (b. 1833) and PETER TCHAIKOVSKY (b. 1840) were both born on this day. (Play one of their beautiful symphonies in celebration of the day.)

8ᵀᴴ   This day marks the birthdate of JEAN HENRI DUNANT, founder of the International Red Cross. (He reversed the colors of his country's flag to create the Red Cross symbol. What country was he from?)

9ᵀᴴ   MOTHER'S DAY was recognized as a national holiday for the first time on this day in 1914. (Students might like to make special Mother's Day cards, for their moms, in celebration.)

10ᵀᴴ   Today is GOLDEN SPIKE DAY! A gold railroad spike was driven into the tracks at Promontory Point, Utah, on this day in 1869. (Ask your students to find out about the significance of this event.)

11TH IRVING BERLIN, American composer and songwriter, was born on this day in 1888. (Lead your class in an enthusiastic rendition of "America the Beautiful.")

12TH British author and inventor of the limerick EDWARD LEAR was born on this day in 1812. (Ask your students to try writing their own clever limericks.)

13TH JOE LEWIS, former heavyweight champion of the world, was born on this day in 1914. (Most boxers have nicknames. Ask your students to read about Joe Lewis and find out his nickname.)

14TH JAMESTOWN, the first English settlement in America, was founded in Virginia on this day in 1607. (Ask a student to locate Jamestown on the class map.)

15TH American children's author LYMAN FRANK BAUM was born on this day in 1856. (Ask your students to find out which books made this author famous.)

16TH WILLIAM HENRY SEWARD, U.S. politician, was born on this day in 1801. He was responsible for acquiring our largest state. (Ask your students to identify this state.)

17TH The first KENTUCKY DERBY was held on this day in 1875. (Ask your students to find out the name of the first winner. Ask them to make up names of horses they might choose if they were racing in the Derby.)

18TH MOUNT ST. HELENS erupted on this day in 1980. (Ask your students to locate the state in which Mount St. Helens is located.)

19TH The first person convicted of a crime on the basis of FINGERPRINTS taken at the scene took place on this day in 1911. (Have each student take his or her own fingerprints and compare them with other children in the class.)

20TH French artist HENRI ROUSSEAU was born on this day in 1844. (Find an art print, or two, of Rousseau's and display it in the classroom.)

21ST CHARLES LINDBERGH successfully completed the first solo transatlantic flight on this day in 1927. (Ask your students to find out the name of his famous plane.)

22ND The author of the "Sherlock Holmes" books, SIR ARTHUR CONAN DOYLE, was born on this day in 1859. (Ask your students to write their own mystery stories in commemoration.)

23RD AMBROSE EVERETT BURNSIDE, U.S. Civil War army general, was born on this day in 1824. (His style of facial whiskers became a fashion trend. Can your students guess what they were called?)

24TH The BROOKLYN BRIDGE opened on this day in 1883. (Ask your students to find out where this bridge is located and what two bodies of land it links.)

25TH The Walt Disney film "The Three Little Pigs" opened on this day in 1933. (Sing along with your class its theme song, "Who's Afraid of the Big Bad Wolf?")

26TH JOHN WAYNE, American movie actor, was born on this day in 1907. He was famous for his many western and war movies. (Ask your students to find out more about this patriotic American.)

27TH Chinese philosopher CONFUCIUS was born on this day in 551 B.C. (Ask your students to find some of his famous sayings or ask them to write their own bits of wisdom.)

28TH JIM THORPE, American Olympic champion, was born on this day in 1888. (Your students may enjoy reading about his life in the school library.)

29TH SIR EDMUND HILLAR, of New Zealand, along with a few tribesmen of Nepal, reached the summit of Mt. Everest on this day in 1953. (Ask a student to locate Mt. Everest on the class map and find out its height.)

30TH The HALL OF FAME FOR GREAT AMERICANS was dedicated on this day at New York University in 1901. (Ask your students to make a list of Americans that they think should be included.)

31ST The first official BICYCLE RACE was held outside of Paris, France, on this day in 1868. (Hold a bicycle rodeo with your students in celebration.)

DON'T FORGET THESE OTHER IMPORTANT HOLIDAYS:

    MOTHER'S DAY   (Second Sunday in May)

    MEMORIAL DAY (Last Monday in May)

    NATIONAL TRANSPORTATION DAY (Second Week of May)

    ALL AMERICAN BUCKLE-UP WEEK (Third Week of May)

May Calendar Header

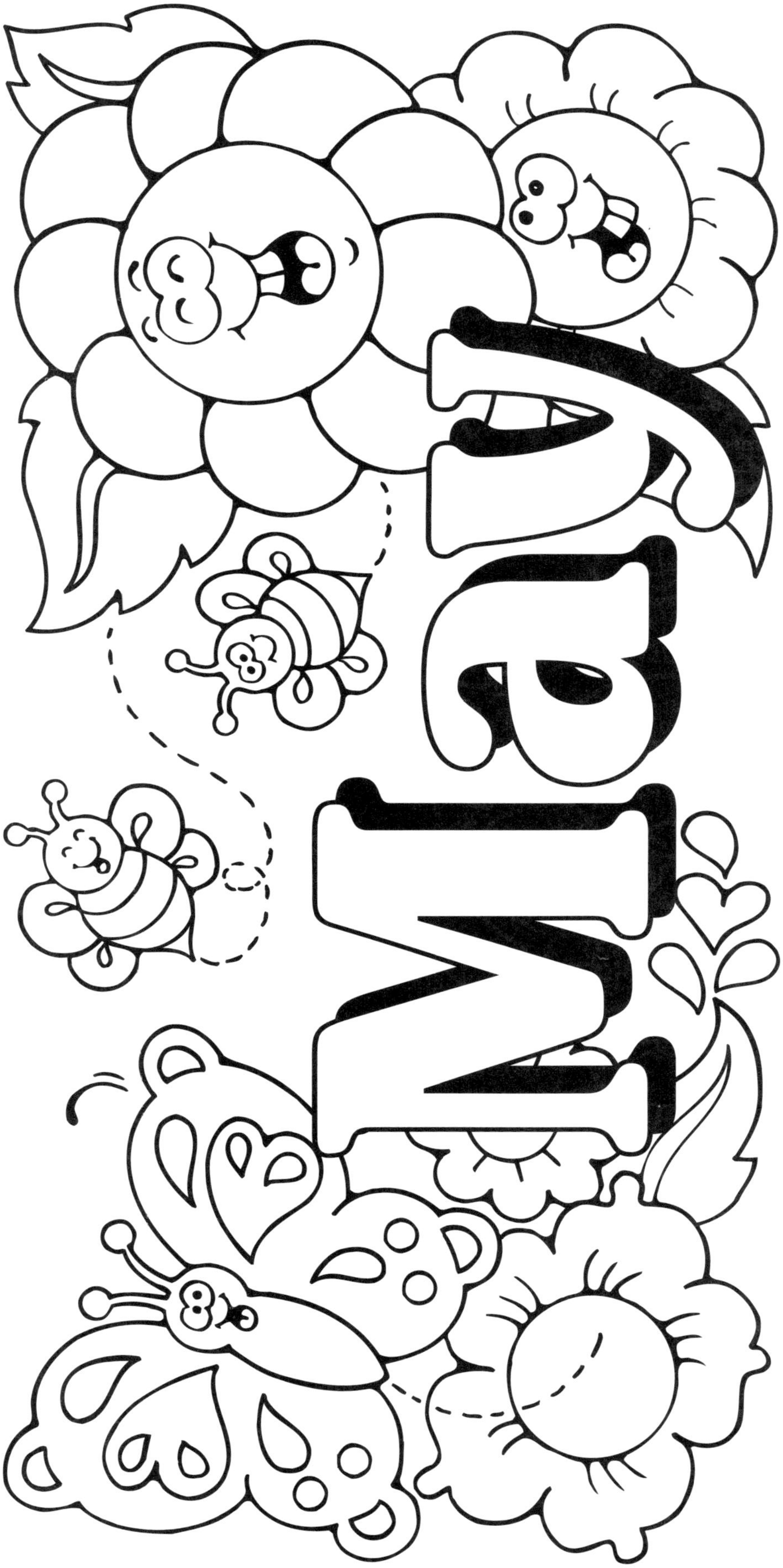

May Calendar Symbols

19

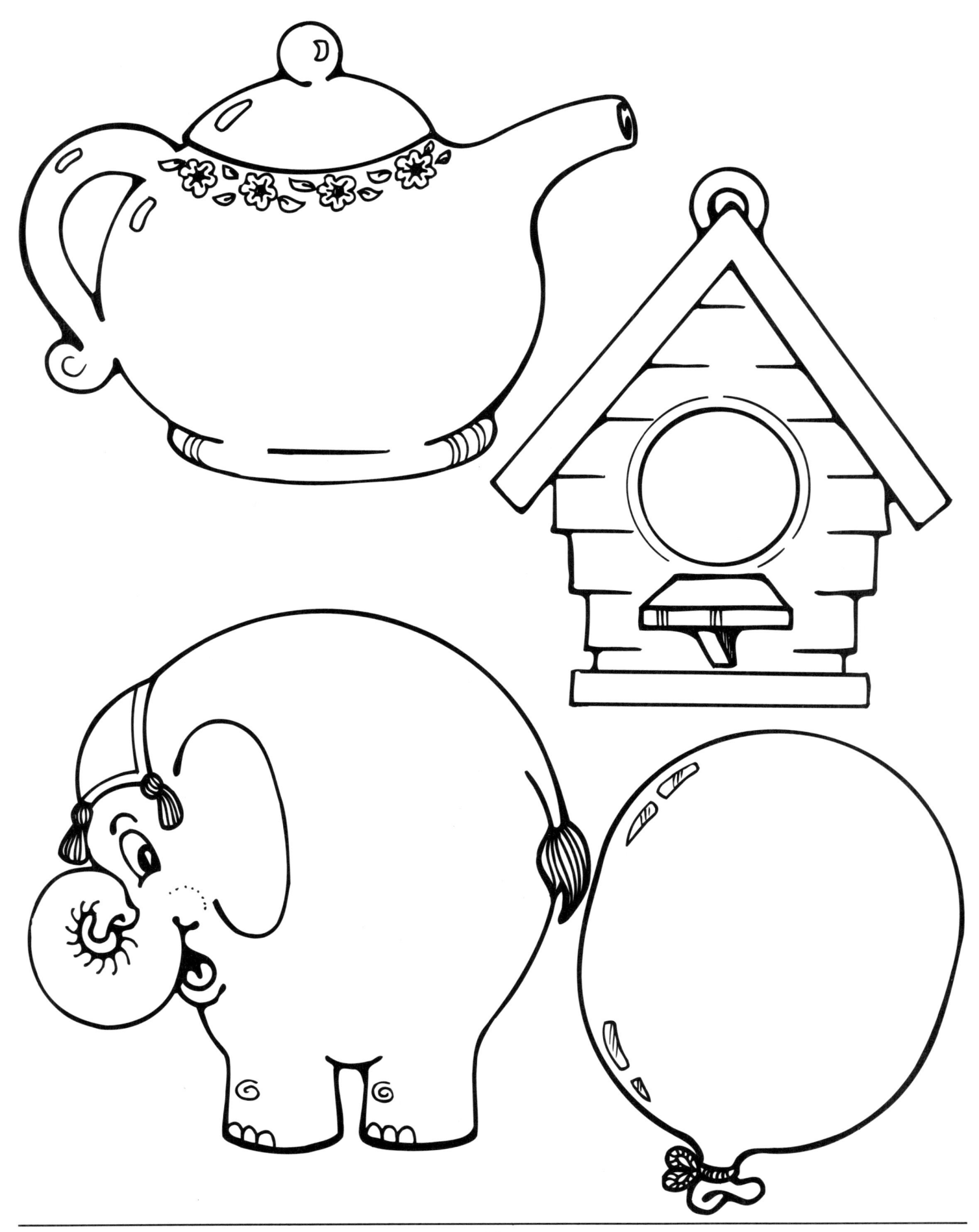

May

Sunday	Monday	Tuesday	Wednesday	Thursday	Friday	Saturday

May Activities!

READ READ READ

Visit the Library and... Read

FLY HIGH AT THE LIBRARY!

Name _____

Really Blossomed Today!

_____
_____

Teacher _____

Date _____

Name _____

was a real joy today!

Teacher _____ Date _____

Name _____

was a perfect young lady today!

Date _____
Teacher _____

Name _____

was a perfect gentleman today!

Date _____
Teacher _____

Teacher's Friend Publications, Inc. ©   23   TF0100 January Idea Book

Pencil Toppers

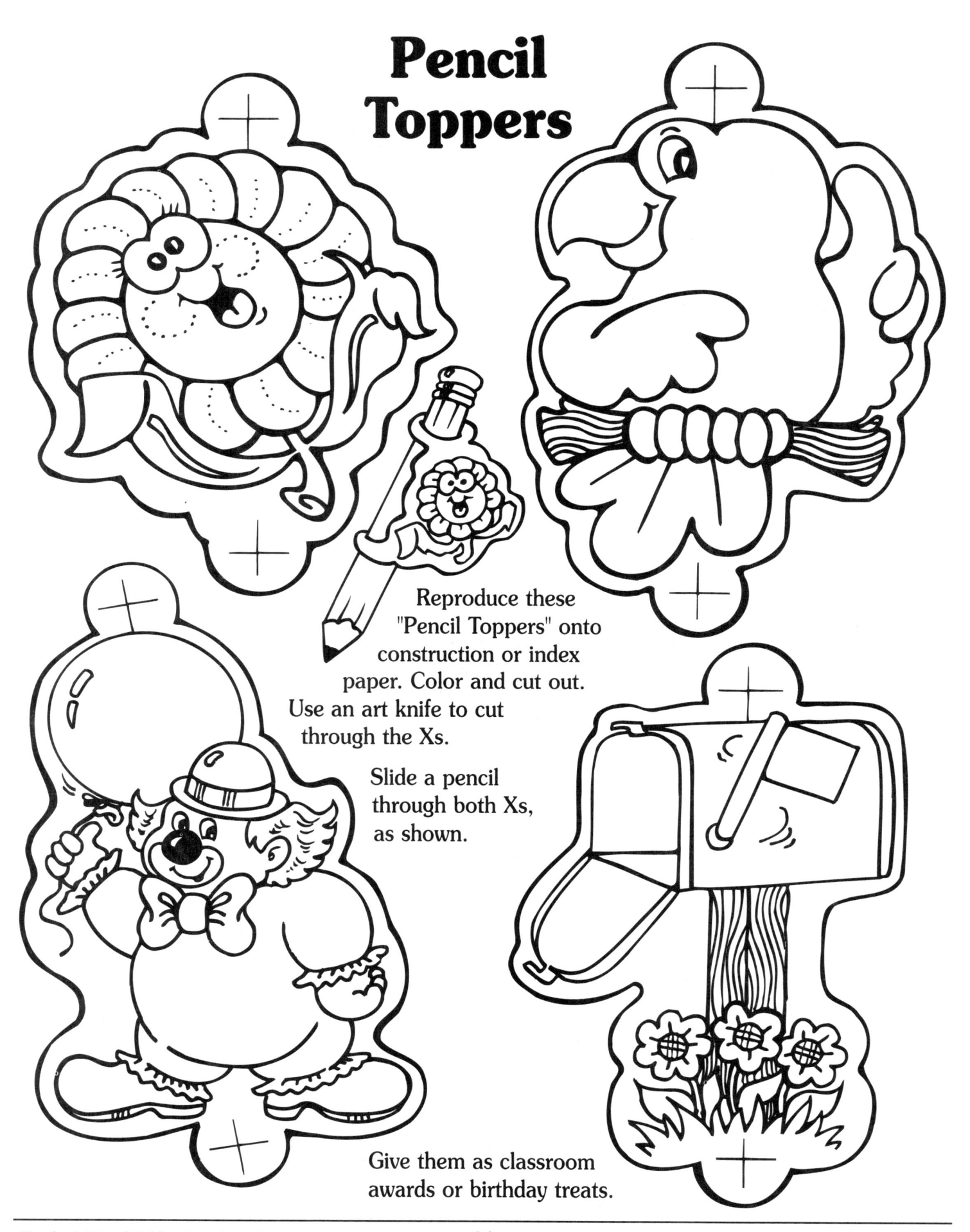

Reproduce these "Pencil Toppers" onto construction or index paper. Color and cut out. Use an art knife to cut through the Xs.

Slide a pencil through both Xs, as shown.

Give them as classroom awards or birthday treats.

Teacher's Friend Publications, Inc. ©   TF0100 January Idea Book

Flower Paper Bag Puppet

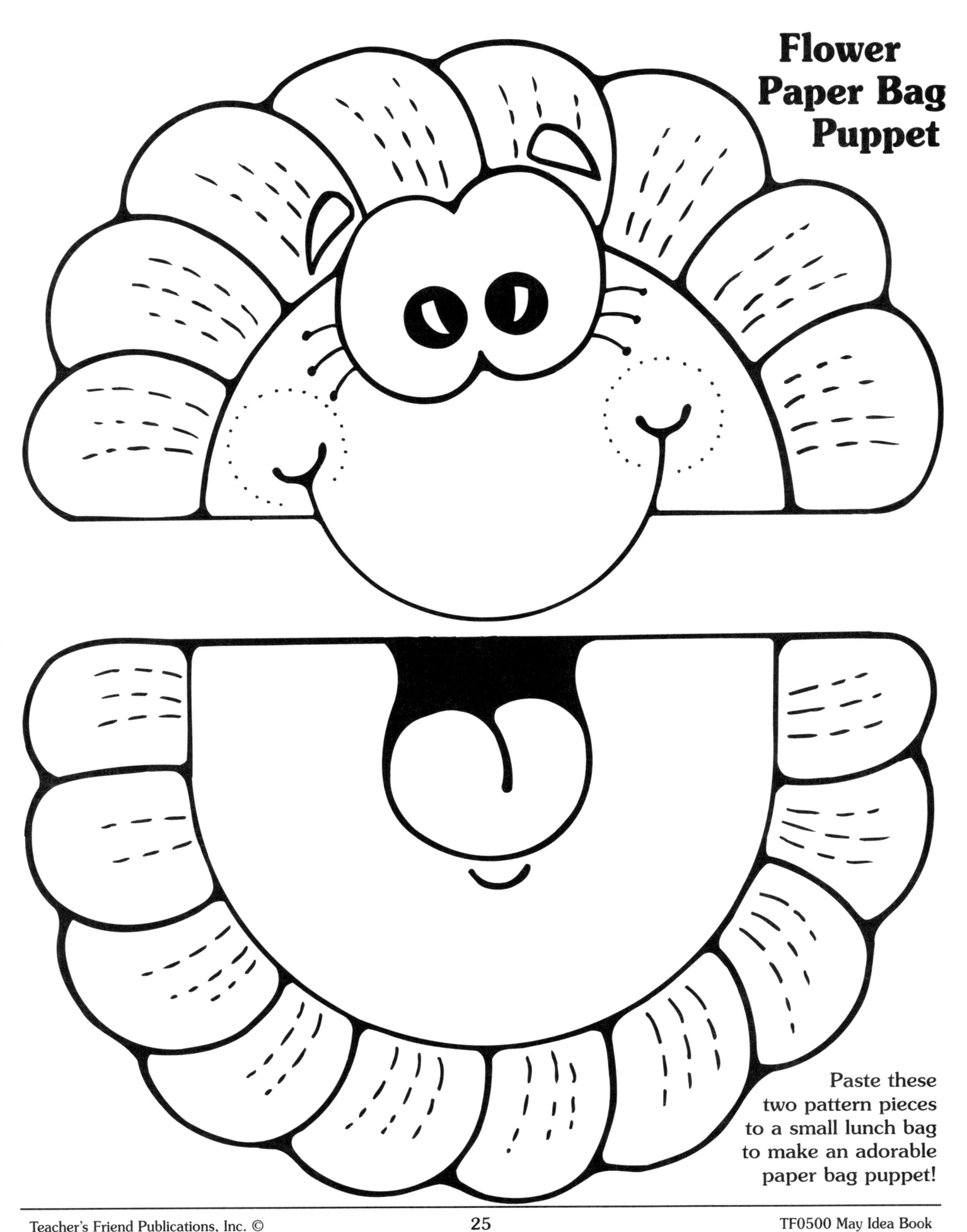

Paste these two pattern pieces to a small lunch bag to make an adorable paper bag puppet!

Teacher's Friend Publications, Inc. © 　　　　25　　　　TF0500 May Idea Book

Flower Patterns

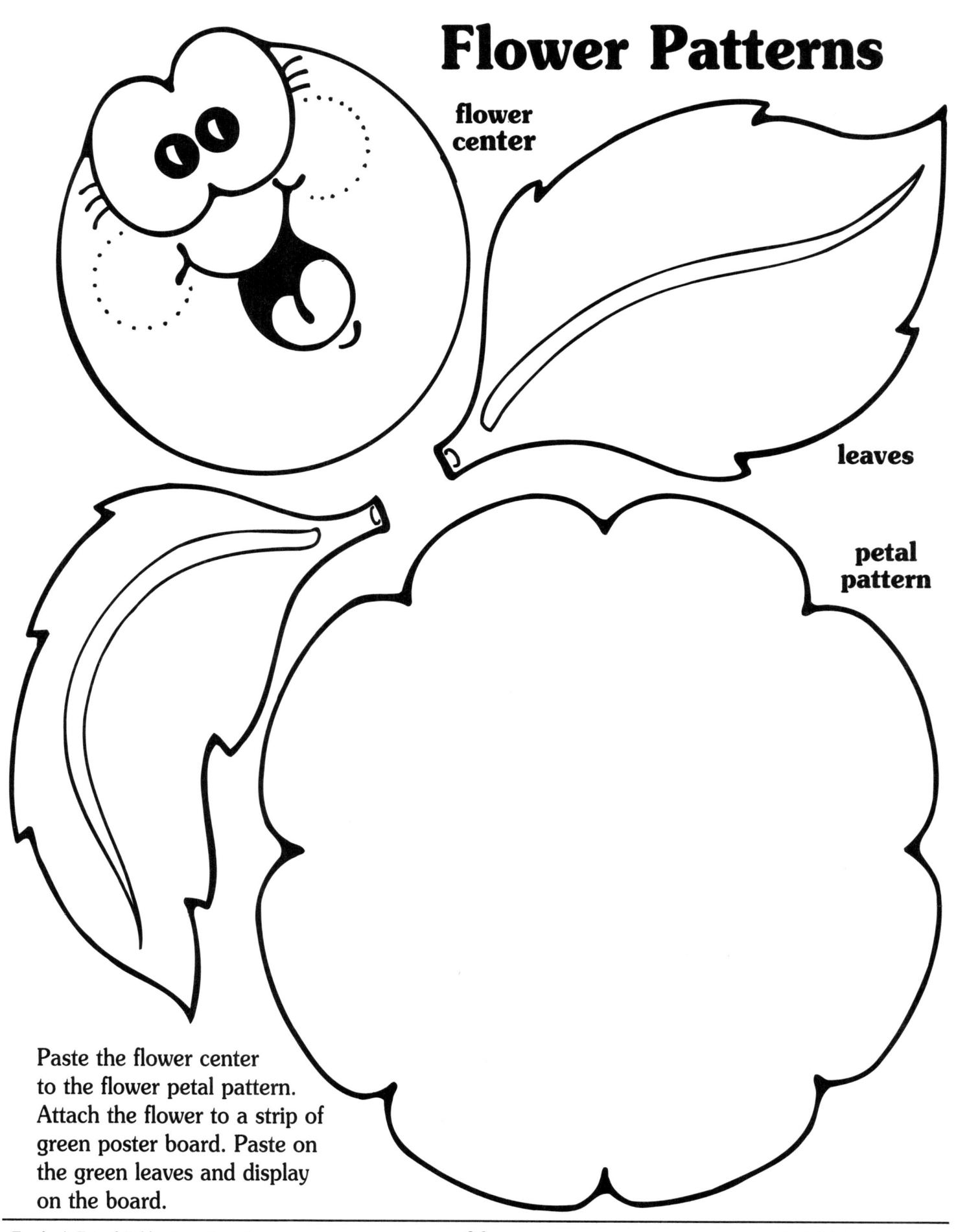

flower center

leaves

petal pattern

Paste the flower center to the flower petal pattern. Attach the flower to a strip of green poster board. Paste on the green leaves and display on the board.

Teacher's Friend Publications, Inc. ©   26   TF0500 May Idea Book

May Booklet Cover

Name

CERTIFICATE OF RECOGNITION

presented to

_____
NAME

in recognition of

_____
_____
_____

_____
TEACHER

_____
DATE

STUDENT
OF THE
MONTH

NAME

SCHOOL

DATE

TEACHER

Teacher's Friend Publications, Inc. ©   29   TF0500 May Idea Book

Field Trip Ideas!

SUGGESTIONS AND IDEAS!
May is a great time for a field trip. There are many places in your own home town that offer wonderful opportunities for a great field trip. Some of these locations may be within walking distance of your school. Some, you will need to provide transportation. Here are some suggestions:

- airport
- art museum
- automotive repair shop
- bakery
- carpentry shop
- college or university
- dairy farm
- dentist's office
- doctor's office
- donut shop
- fire station
- fish market
- florist
- grocery store
- historic home
- horse stable
- ice cream parlor
- library
- manufacturing plant
- movie theater

- museum
- musical instrument store
- newspaper office
- park
- pet store
- photography studio
- pizza shop
- police station
- print shop
- radio station
- recycling center
- radio station
- retirement home
- telephone company
- television station
- tree nursery
- train station
- utility company
- veterinary clinic
- planetarium

When planning the field trip, make sure you give the proprietors at least two weeks notice. Tell them the age of your students and what types of things you wish them to see and experience. Here are some suggestions:

Bakery: Let the baker know that you would like the students to see the different stages of baking bread followed by having them sample a freshly baked loaf.

Pizza Shop: Suggest that the proprietor show the students the various supplies and ovens needed for making pizza. He or she may even let the students add their own toppings to a pizza they make themselves.

Remind shopkeepers that by having your class visit their establishment, a connection to their homes is made. Children will eagerly ask their parents to visit the particular shops they have visited on the class field trip.

Field trips to local establishments also reinforce the variety of career choices available to students as they grow older.

Field Trip Ideas!

ORGANIZATIONAL IDEAS:
- Before leaving on the trip, explain all rules and your expectations to your students. On the class board, write a list of things you wish them to observe and experience. Discuss these things with your students.
- Have students wear name tags, headbands or visors while on the field trip.
- Ask students to all wear the same color T-shirt.
- Provide parent helpers and the bus driver with matching name tags.
- Give the bus driver and each group leader a list of the students' names for quick reference.
- Ask a parent to videotape the entire field trip. Show the film during Parent Night or show it to the children the next day in class followed by a class discussion.
- The day before, have students decorate small lunch bags. Instruct parents to pack simple lunches for their children (including a drink in a disposable container) in the bags.
- Have the leader or chaperone of each group wear a funny hat or hold a colorful umbrella. The children can easily find their group by simply by looking for the leader.
- Take a field trip kit with you on the excursion. It should include: safety pins, Band-Aids®, paper towels, plastic bags, disposable wipes, a few dollars worth of change, bottles of water and disposable cups and a list of students' emergency phone numbers, including the numbers of your school and principal.
- The day after, have students write thank you notes to the people they met during the field trip.

Name Tag

We're on a Field Trip!

Student's Name

School

Teacher

Teacher's Friend Publications, Inc. ©   TF0500 May Idea Book

We're Going On a Field Trip!

The class of _____

in room# _____   will be going

on a field trip to: _____.

Place: _____

Date: _____

Time Leaving: _____ Time Returning: _____

Please make sure your child: _____

_____

Comments: _____

_____

**Return the signed Permission Slip to your child's teacher.
(Without this signed form your child cannot attend.)**

Field Trip
PERMISSSION SLIP

I give my permission for _____

to go on the field trip to _____

on _____.

Comments: _____

_____

Signed _____ _____
            Parent or Guardian   Date

Teacher's Friend Publications, Inc. ©   TF0500 May Idea Book

My Field Trip Record

Student's Name _____

Destination _____

Date _____

What we did... _____

_____

_____

_____

What we saw... _____

_____

_____

_____

What we learned... _____

_____

_____

_____

I liked or disliked the trip because... _____

_____

_____

_____

Field Trip Visor

Copy this Field Trip Visor onto sturdy index or construction paper. Children can do the coloring.

Punch holes at both ends and attach string elastic or mailing string. (With elastic, the students can easily remove the visors without retying.)

Name

School

I'M ON A FIELD TRIP!

May Day!

May Day - May 1st!

The spring festival known in many countries as May Day is observed on May 1st. This holiday acknowledges the rebirth and revival of life that the spring season brings after the harsh, cold winter.

In ancient times, the Romans offered bouquets of flowers to Flora, their goddess of spring. They called the festival Floralia. As the Romans inhabited more of Europe during the Middle Ages, they took their May Day customs with them. In medieval English villages, people gathered flowers and blooming tree branches to decorate their homes and churches. It was called "bringing in the May!" They also picked small bouquets of flowers early in the morning and secretly left them on friends' or relatives' doorsteps. Later in the day, the people of the village would gather at the town square and raise the Maypole. The pole was often more than 100 feet tall with numerous brightly colored streamers attached to the top. After the Maypole was in place, dancers would each take hold of a streamer and circle the pole, dancing and weaving the ribbons into intricate patterns. When the dancers changed direction, the streamers would fall free and dance would begin again. The festivities included the crowning of the May Queen. In many towns of Europe and some places in America, this tradition has continued.

In 1889, a group of French socialists dedicated May 1st to the working people. This holiday, Labor Day, or International Workers' Day, is observed by many nations and resembles the September holiday in the Untied States. The government and labor organizations of these countries sponsor parades and other celebrations to honor the working class people.

May Day was extremely important in Communist countries. For the people of the Union of Soviet Socialist Republics (U.S.S.R.), this was a day for special parties and celebrations. All businesses were closed and an impressive military parade through Red Square was the highlight of the day.

ACTIVITIES:
Make your own Maypole by attaching long ribbons or crepe paper streamers to the top of the school flag pole or tether ball pole. Let groups of children take turns dancing around the pole and weaving the streamers into fun designs.

The day before, encourage your students to rise early in the morning of May 1st and pick a small bouquet of flowers that can be left secretly for their mom or other family member. If real flowers are hard to come by, have students make paper flowers to give on May Day.

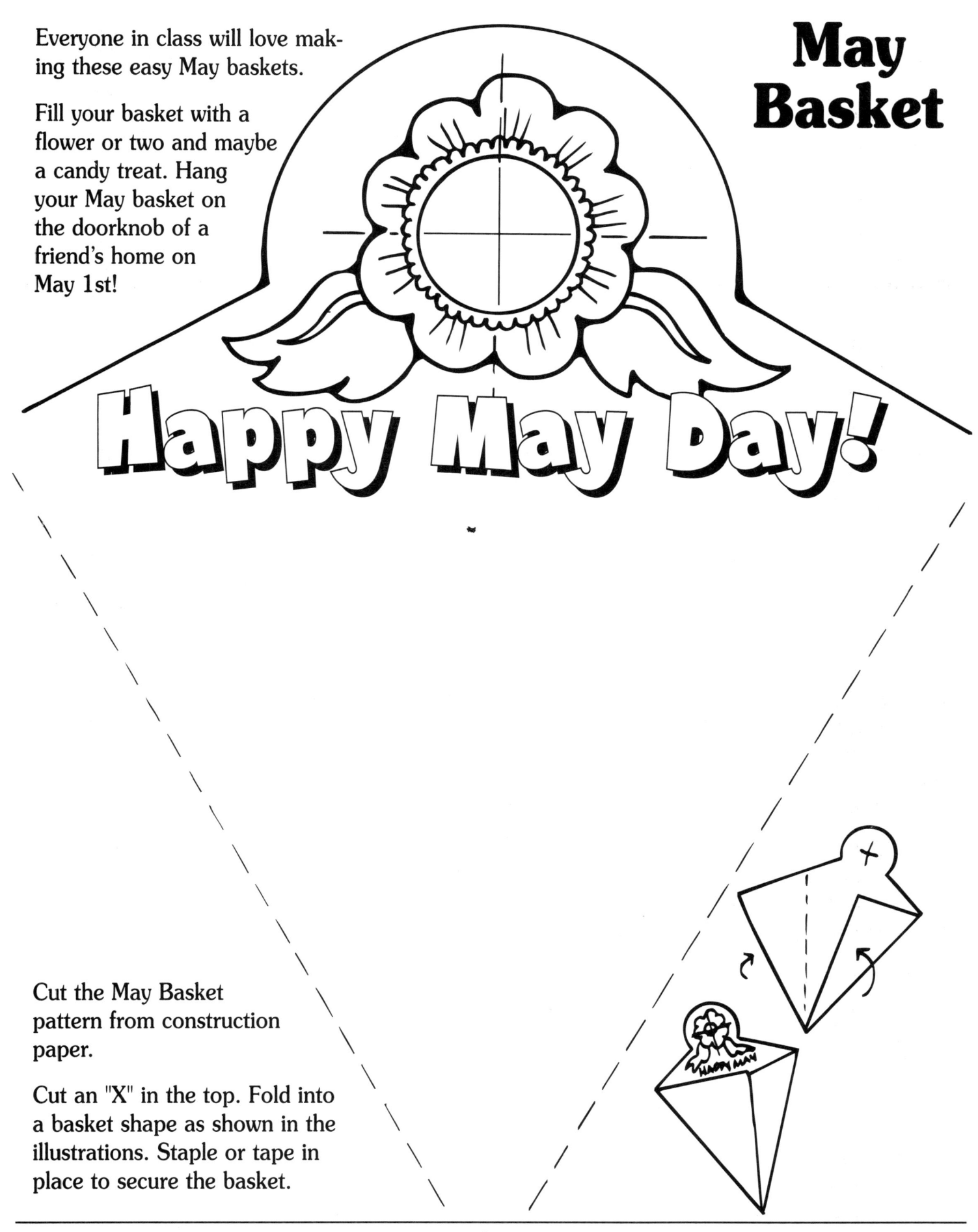

Everyone in class will love making these easy May baskets.

Fill your basket with a flower or two and maybe a candy treat. Hang your May basket on the doorknob of a friend's home on May 1st!

May Basket

Happy May Day!

Cut the May Basket pattern from construction paper.

Cut an "X" in the top. Fold into a basket shape as shown in the illustrations. Staple or tape in place to secure the basket.

Teacher's Friend Publications, Inc. © TF0500 May Idea Book

International Children

Russia

International Children

Russia

FOLD

Mini Flower Booklets

Copy these flower booklets onto brightly colored paper. Have students write May Day poems inside.

Display the flowers on the class bulletin board along with paper stems and leaves.

FOLD

Teacher's Friend Publications, Inc. © 40 TF0500 May Idea Book

These mini flower booklet patterns can also make beautiful Mother's Day cards!

Flower booklets can also be enlarged for a more dramatic display!

FOLD

FOLD

Teacher's Friend Publications, Inc. © 41 TF0500 May Idea Book

My Flower Report

Student's Name

The flower I've chosen is:
_____

My flower comes in these colors:
_____ _____

_____ _____

My flower grows best in:
_____

_____

Picture of my flower!

Directions for planting seeds:
_____

_____

_____

_____

Here is a poem about my flower!
_____

_____

_____

_____

Matching Flower Pots

Several matching activities can easily be made by making several flowers and flower pots from colored construction paper. For a math activity, label each flower with a problem and the flower pots with appropriate answers. Long and short vowel sounds can be practiced with the same type of matching activity. Label each flower with a short or long vowel. Write words appropriate to the sounds on the flower pots and have students match them to the flowers. (Remember to have students work on only one or two vowel sounds at a time.)

Cut

Plants and Flowers!

Use the inspiration of May Day to teach your students about the importance of plants and flowers to our lives. Human and animal life could not exist without plants.

Plants take in water and minerals from the soil and carbon dioxide from the air. Sunlight, which gives a plant energy, is absorbed through the leaves and allows the plant to process these elements into oxygen. This process of changing inorganic matter into organic matter is called "*photosynthesis.*" Because of this process, we have plenty of oxygen to breathe and live.

One of the most vital functions of plants is to provide a source of food. Birds, fish, insects, (and, of course, all animals and humans) rely on plants for food, in one way or another.

Plants come in many different shapes, sizes and colors. The tiniest one-cell plant is algae, which can only be seen with a microscope. At over 300 feet high, California redwood trees are the largest plants.

Some plants grow in shady, moist environments, while others thrive in the hot, dry, desert heat. All plants have qualities that make them different from other plants. Some have fragrant leaves or flowers. Others have gorgeous blooms of vibrant colors. Many produce fruit, berries or seeds that are used in a variety of ways. Plants provide fiber for textile industries and essential ingredients for medicines and drugs. Our very homes could not be built without plants.

Whatever type of plant or seed you wish to grow, the experience is sure to be a rewarding one. Try one or more of the following activities.

EGGSHELL PLANTERS

Use eggshell halves as containers for planting seeds in your classroom.

Poke a small hole in the bottom of each eggshell half and place them in an egg carton. Place a small amount of soil in each shell and plant a tomato seed in each one. Mist the seeds with water regularly. When the plants become reasonably large, transplant them outdoors, shell and all!

EASTER GRASS

Grass is easy to grow right in your own Easter basket!

Line a basket with plastic or make your own basket using a plastic milk jug. Fill the basket with vermiculite, a mineral substance available at most plant nurseries. Next, sprinkle wheat seed over the vermiculite and water until moist. (Don't water again for at least a week.) Set the basket in a sunny window and cover with plastic wrap for 48 hours. In a few days, the wheat seed will begin to sprout, and in no time at all, a miniature meadow will be ready for your Easter eggs!

Plants and Flowers!

VEGETABLE SOUP

Introduce your students to a variety of new and different vegetables with this yummy activity.

Ask each student to bring in one or two vegetables from home. (You might wish to bring in a few yourself, such as zucchini, parsnips, cabbage or mushrooms.) Instruct your students in peeling and cutting up the vegetables. Discuss which vegetables are plant roots and which are leaves. Place all of the cut vegetables in a large pot of water and add bouillon and salt for flavor. Cook over a low heat, for most of the day.

The children will love sampling a vegetable soup they made themselves.

BEAN CONTEST

Conduct a class "Bean Growing Contest" in which everyone will love to compete.

Have each participant fill a milk carton, which has been cut in half, with soil. Ask them to plant five or six beans in the soil. Tell the students that they may do anything they wish to get their beans to grow faster and better. They must, however, keep a daily log of the plant's environment and care. At the end of six weeks, compare the plants. Award the student with the best looking plant a "Green Thumb" Award! (Use the daily logs in a discussion about the care of growing plants.)

FLOWER POWER

Provide a flower for every child in class and ask them these questions:

How many petals does your flower have? Does your flower have a fragrance? What purpose do you think the flower serves?

Can you carefully take apart your flower and identify its parts?
    Petals   Pistil
    Stamen   Sepal
    Stem   Leaves

Is there pollen inside your flower?

What type of insect might be attracted to your flower? How does your flower look under a magnifying glass?

Teacher: One of the best flowers to use for this exercise is a daffodil.

GROWING SEEDS

With this simple activity, seeds quickly grow right in your classroom!

Place one or two handfuls of potting soil in zip-lock bags that you have given to each child. Ask them to gently place three or four seeds in the soil. (Beans work especially well.) Sprinkle a few drops of water in the bags and seal. Have each student label the bag with his/her name and tape it to the class window. In three or four days, students will observe tiny sprouts and roots beginning to form. There is no need to water the new plants, so do not open the bags until the sprouts are large enough to transplant.

Parts of a Flower

Label these flower parts: petal, pistil, stamen, sepal, stem

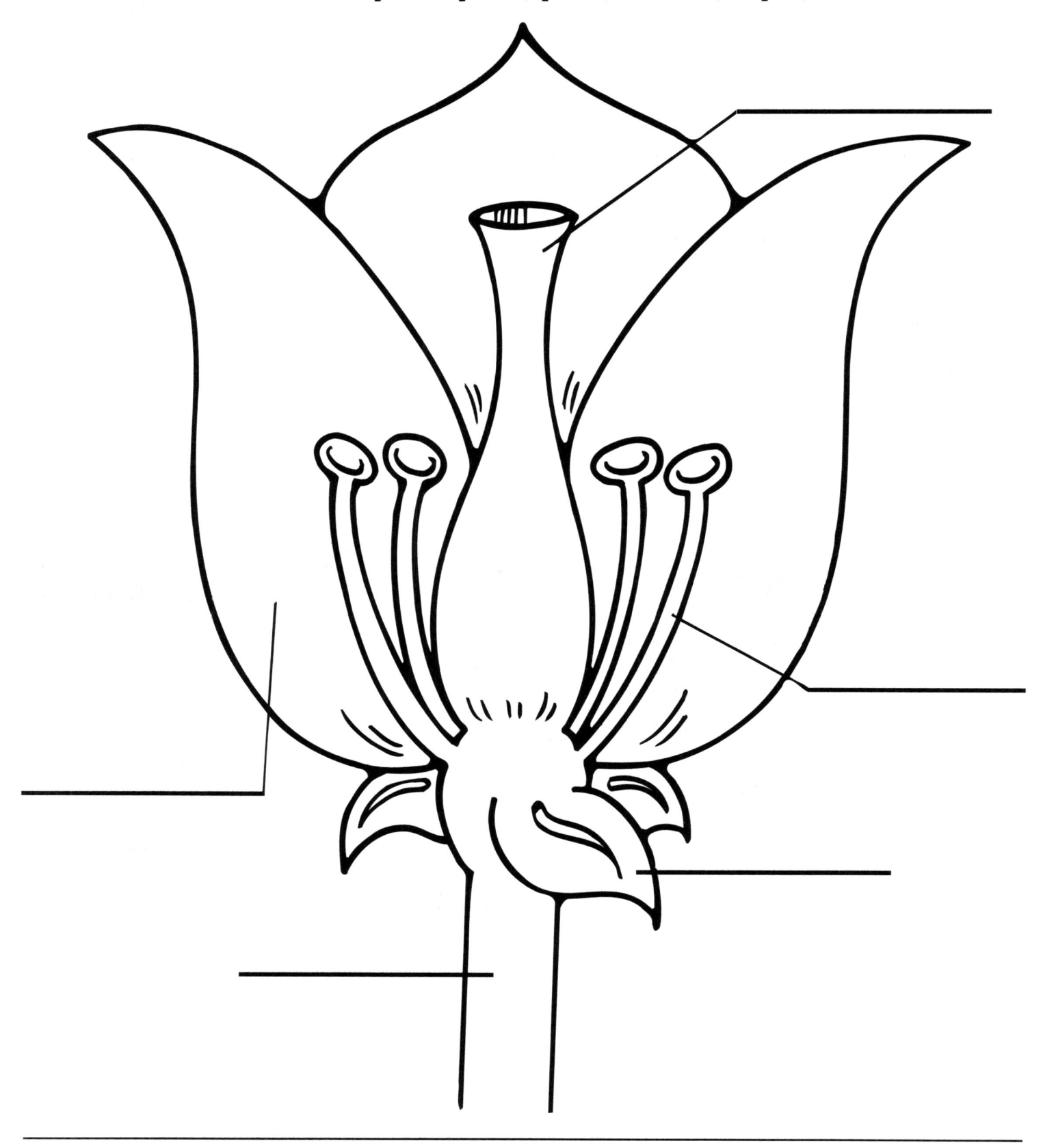

Plants and Flowers!

PLANT MARKERS

Make markers for your students' plants by cutting this flower pattern from construction or index paper. Children can write their own names and the names of their plants on the center of each flower.

Fold the spike along the dotted lines and place it in the soil at the base of the plant.

Plant markers can also be used as gift tags for Easter or Mother's Day!

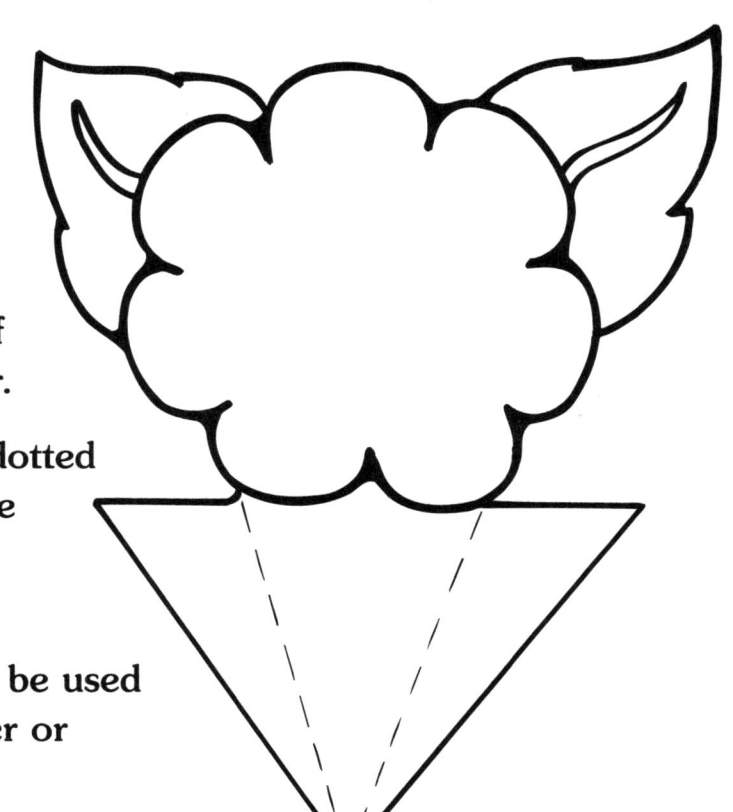

Green Thumb Award

This is to recognize

_____

who has demonstrated

_____

_____

Date _____ **Teacher** _____

Growing Flower

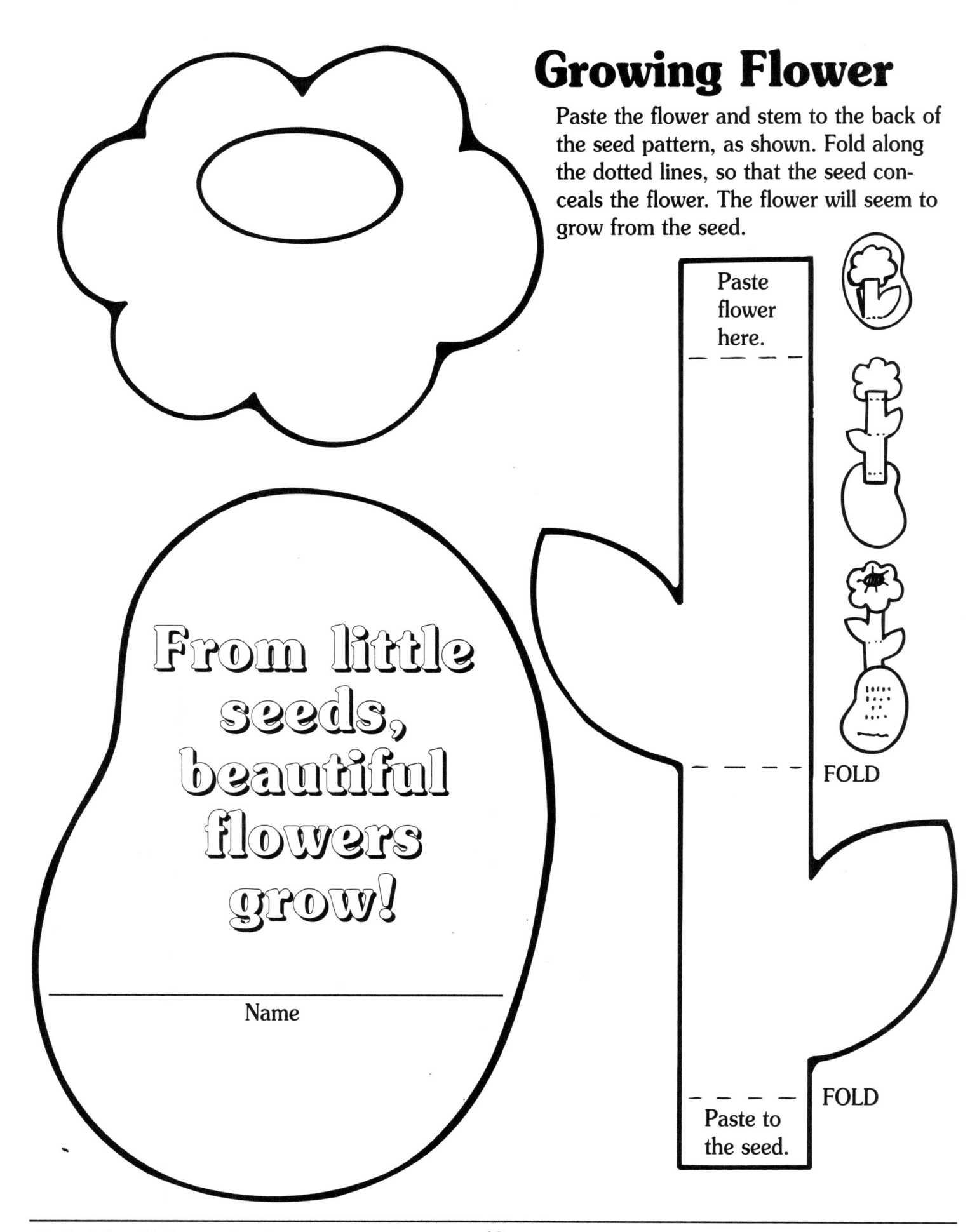

Paste the flower and stem to the back of the seed pattern, as shown. Fold along the dotted lines, so that the seed conceals the flower. The flower will seem to grow from the seed.

Paste flower here.

FOLD

FOLD

Paste to the seed.

From little seeds, beautiful flowers grow!

Name

Teacher's Friend Publications, Inc. © 48 TF0500 May Idea Book

My Garden Book

_____
Name

Planting Seeds

I have decided to plant this type of seeds:

_____

Date I planted my seeds: _____

My plant will grow to be about this tall: _____

Here are the directions to plant my seeds:

_____

_____

_____

My plant will be a: ☐ flower   ☐ vegetable
                        ☐ fruit   ☐ herb
                                    ☐ other

Plants needs water!

My watering schedule:

Sun.	Mon.	Tues.	Wed.	Thurs.	Fri.	Sat.

Check off each day you water your plant.

I am learning a great deal about plants. I have labeled the different plant parts.

Plant Parts Definitions

Leaf _____
Flower _____
Stem _____
Bud _____
Roots _____

I've made sure my plant receives plenty of sunshine! These are the special needs of my plant! _____
_____
_____

A drawing of my plant after 2 weeks.

A drawing of my plant after 4 weeks.

A drawing of my plant after 6 weeks.

A drawing of my plant fully grown.

My plant was this tall on these dates:

Dates	Plant Heighth
_____	_____
_____	_____
_____	_____
_____	_____
_____	_____

After my plant is grown, I will:

_____

_____

_____

_____

Here is a list of six words that describe my plant.

1. _____
2. _____
3. _____
4. _____
5. _____
6. _____

Teacher's Friend Publications, Inc. ©

Repeat Patterns

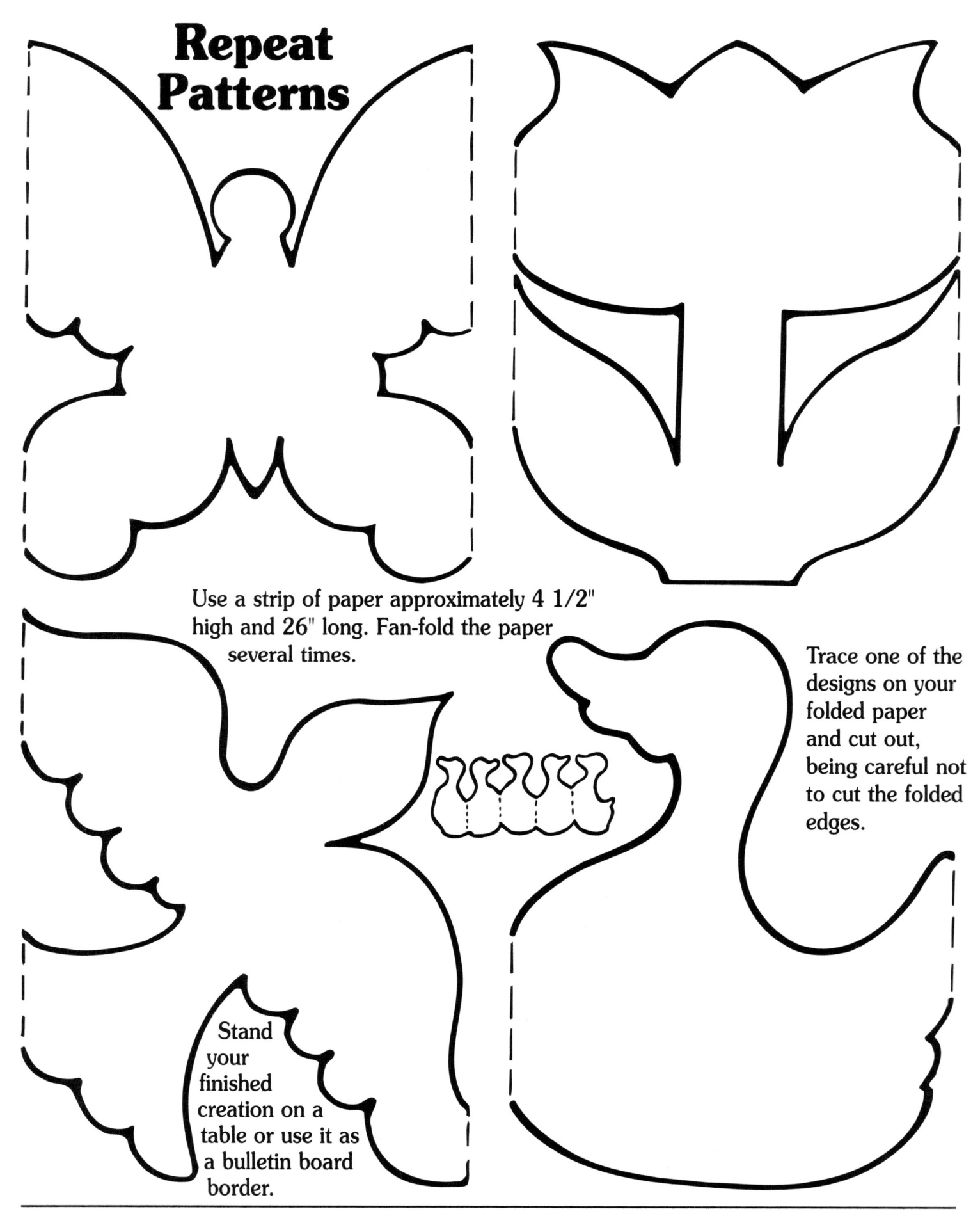

Use a strip of paper approximately 4 1/2" high and 26" long. Fan-fold the paper several times.

Trace one of the designs on your folded paper and cut out, being careful not to cut the folded edges.

Stand your finished creation on a table or use it as a bulletin board border.

Teacher's Friend Publications, Inc. ©   TF0500 May Idea Book

Mother's Day!

Mother's Day - 2nd Sunday in May

In May of 1905, Miss Anna M. Jarvis encouraged her church in Grafton, West Virginia to dedicate a church service in honor of her mother, who had passed away three years before. Because her mother had loved carnations, Anna presented everyone in attendance with one of her special flowers. Red carnations were given to honor mothers who were living and white carnations for those who had passed on.

The following year, Miss Jarvis campaigned to have a special day declared in honor of all mothers. She began her campaign by writing letters to members of Congress and other important people. Several states soon declared a "Mother's Day," usually celebrated on a Sunday in the month of May. Carnations continued to be associated with this special day.

On May 9, 1914, President Woodrow Wilson announced the first Mother's Day Proclamation. The second Sunday in May was set aside for this occasion. President Wilson proclaimed that Mother's Day should be observed to express "our love and reverence for the mothers of our country."

Today, Mother's Day is still celebrated in churches and homes throughout America. It is a day in which special attention is given to all mothers and grandmothers. Cards and gifts are often given along with bouquets or corsages of carnations. Many families treat mom with a special breakfast or dinner out in a favorite restaurant.

Mother's Day is celebrated on different dates and times in many parts of the world. In every case, it is a time of gratitude and remembrance, a time to express love and appreciation.

Give Mom this special Mother's Day badge to show how much you appreciate her.

Color and decorate the badge with glitter or sequins. Add a real satin bow to the top if you wish.

Happy Mother's Day!

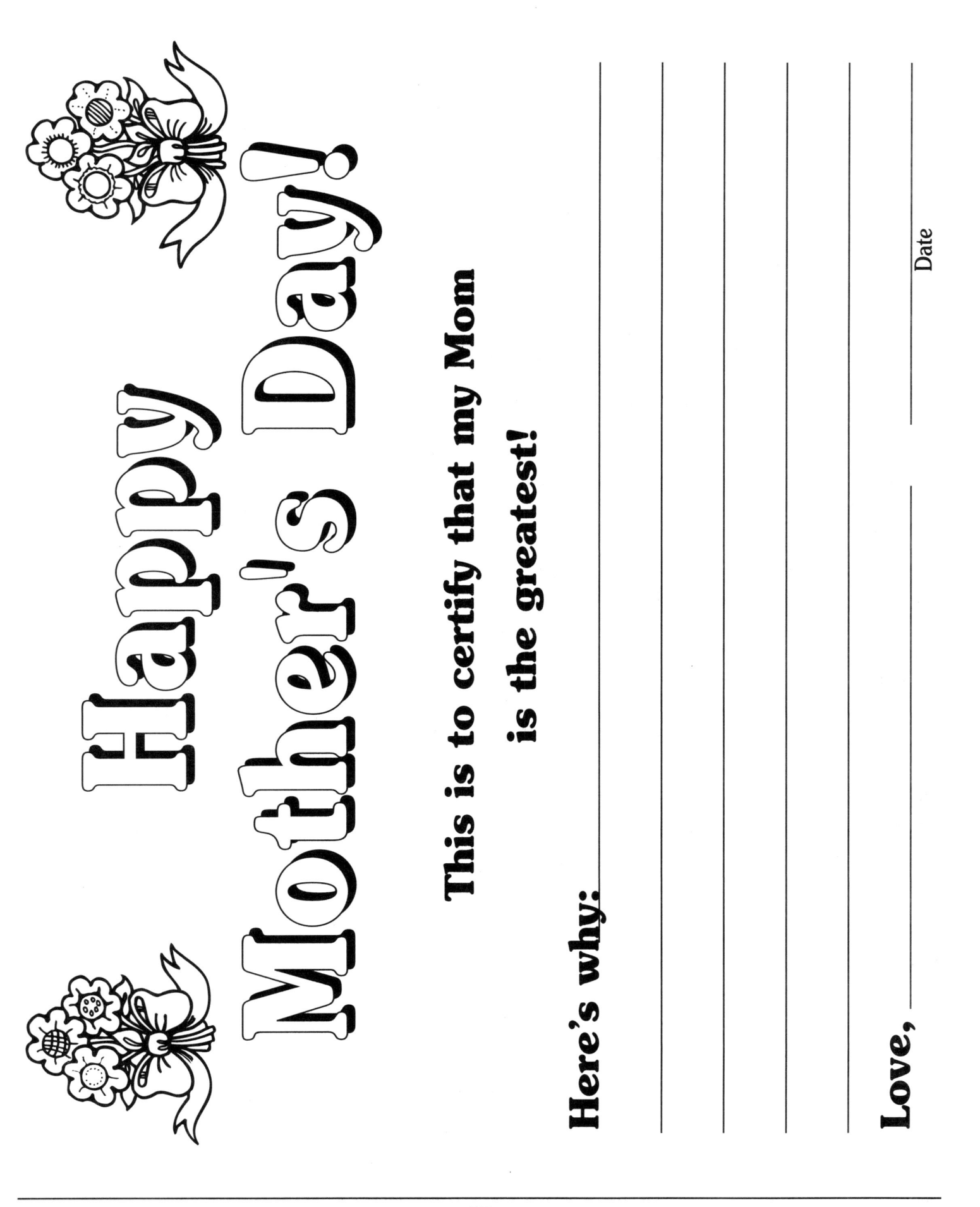

This is to certify that my Mom

is the greatest!

Here's why: _____

_____

_____

_____

_____ Date

Love, _____

Teacher's Friend Publications, Inc. ©   57   TF0500 May Idea Book

To: My Mom!

My Special Mother's Day Pledge!

As my gift to you for Mother's Day, I promise to...

1. _____

2. _____

3. _____

4. _____

5. _____

With all my love!

_____

Mother's Day Crafts!

MOM'S MINI SEWING KIT

Remove the staples and insides of a matchbook. Open it out flat and glue a piece of bright gift wrap to the outside.

Cut a small piece of poster board that will fit inside the matchbook. Wrap several different colors of thread around the cardboard and place it in the matchbook. A small piece of felt containing a few straight pins and a needle or two should also be included. Staple the matchbook together to hold everything in place.

SCENTED SACHETS

Cut an eight-inch square of nylon netting. Place a cotton ball in the center of the netting and sprinkle with scented powder or cologne. Gather the four corners of the netting together and tie with a pretty ribbon. Mom will love having this sachet to hang in her closet or place in her dresser drawer.

MOTHER'S DAY BOOKMARKS

Cotton fabric can be laminated to make delightful bookmarks. After laminating the fabric, cut it into 2" x 6" strips. Punch a hole in one end of the bookmark and add a colorful yarn tassel.

Mom will love using her new bookmark while reading her favorite novel.

Teacher's Friend Publications, Inc. ©   TF0500 May Idea Book

Mother's Day Crafts!

HANDPRINTS IN THE SAND

Supply a plastic tub of moist sand and have each child take turns pressing his or her hand into the sand. Make sure each child makes a deep, clear impression.

Pour a thick mixture of plaster into the impression and allow it to dry. Carefully remove the print and brush the excess sand away. (Footprints are also fun to make the same way.)

These hand prints make wonderful paper weights for Mom on Mother's Day.

HAND SPRAY

Mix a thin mixture of water and tempera paint and pour it into an empty atomizer bottle. Ask a child to place his or her hand on a sheet of paper and spray the hand with paint.

When the child removes the hand, a silhouette will appear against the spattered paper. Children can easily wash up with soap and water.

COLORFUL HANDPRINTS

Ask each child to paint the palm of their hand with thick poster paint. Have them carefully press their hand onto construction paper. Children might like to repeat the handprint several times with different colors.

Mom will love receiving this colorful reminder of her child's early years.

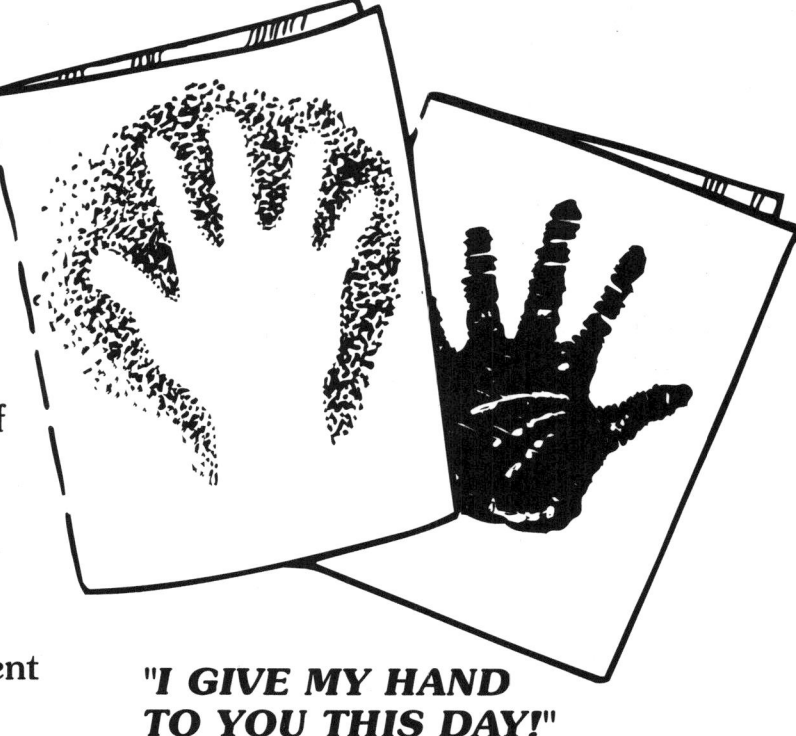

"I GIVE MY HAND TO YOU THIS DAY!"

REMEMBER ME NOW, AS I GROW AND PLAY!"

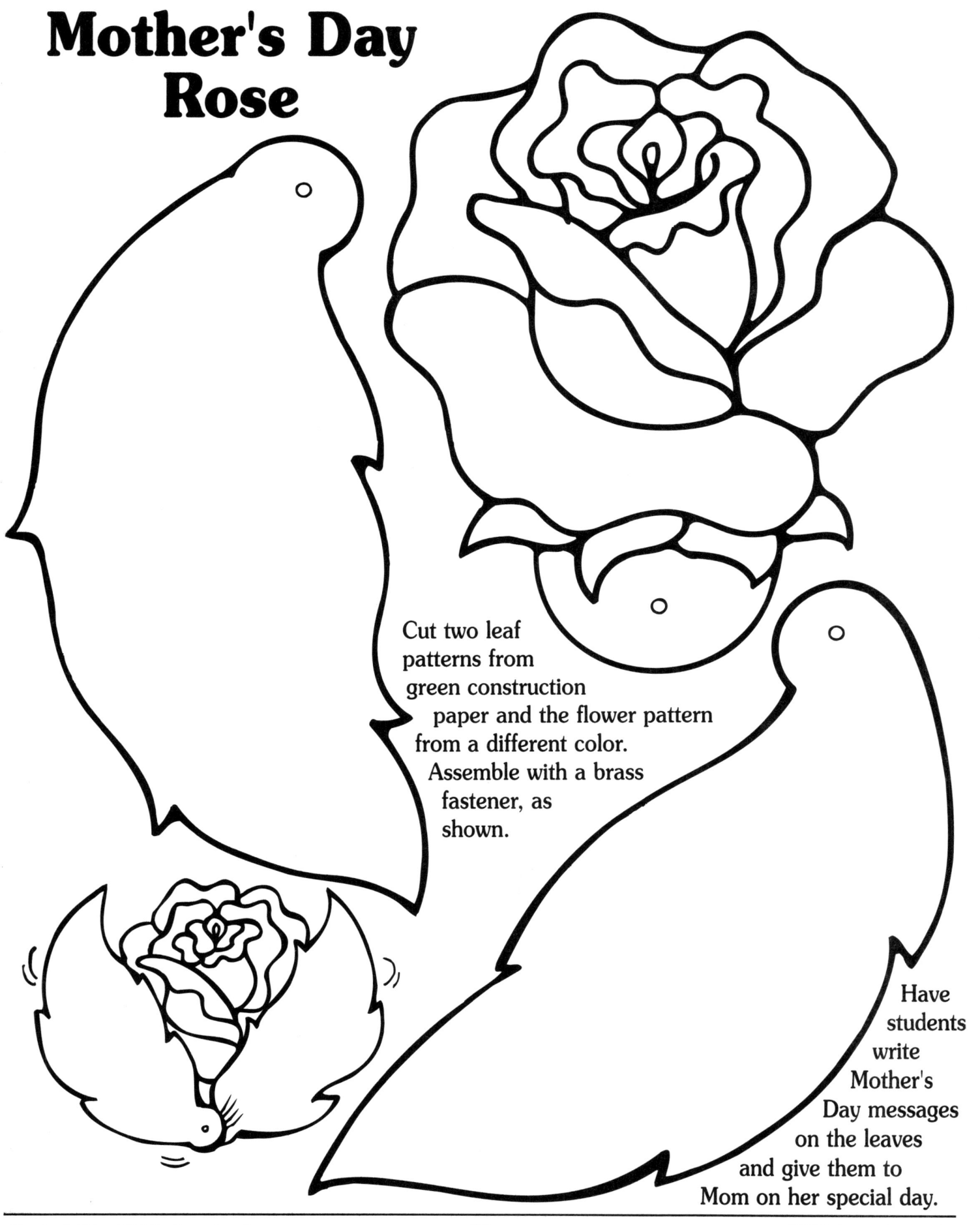

Mother's Day Rose

Cut two leaf patterns from green construction paper and the flower pattern from a different color. Assemble with a brass fastener, as shown.

Have students write Mother's Day messages on the leaves and give them to Mom on her special day.

Teacher's Friend Publications, Inc. ©   63   TF0500 May Idea Book

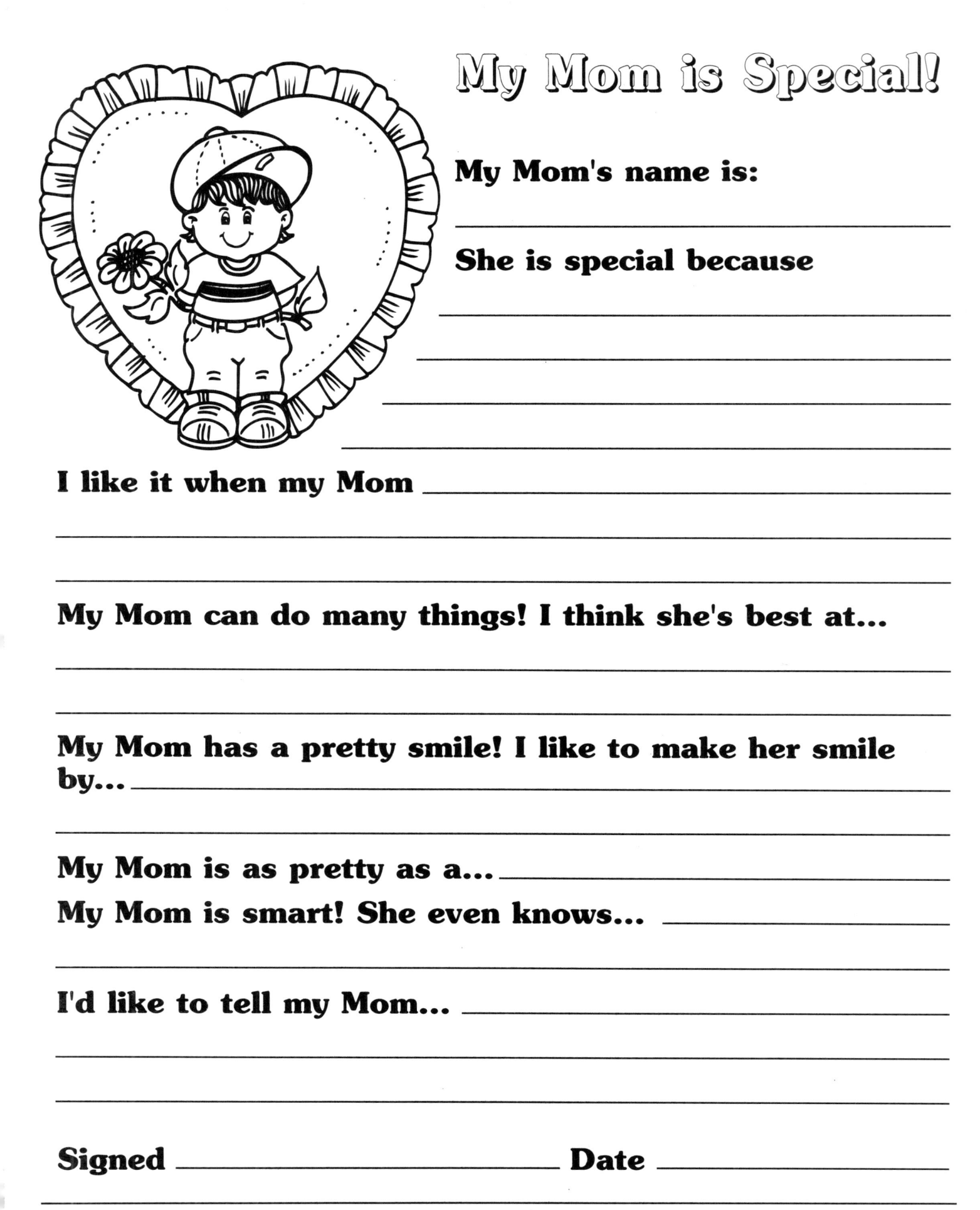

My Mom is Special!

My Mom's name is:
_____

She is special because _____
_____
_____
_____

I like it when my Mom _____
_____
_____

My Mom can do many things! I think she's best at...
_____
_____

My Mom has a pretty smile! I like to make her smile by... _____
_____

My Mom is as pretty as a... _____

My Mom is smart! She even knows... _____
_____

I'd like to tell my Mom... _____
_____
_____

Signed _____ **Date** _____

My Mom is Special!

My Mom's name is:
_____

She is special because
_____
_____
_____

I like it when my Mom _____
_____

My Mom can do many things! I think she's best at...
_____
_____

My Mom has a pretty smile! I like to make her smile by... _____
_____

My Mom is as pretty as a... _____

My Mom is smart! She even knows... _____

I'd like to tell my Mom... _____
_____
_____

Signed _____ **Date** _____

Teacher's Friend Publications, Inc. ©   TF0500 May Idea Book

Mother's Day Creative Writing

Write a word, poem or sentence using each letter in the word M-O-T-H-E-R!

M

O

T

H

E

R

My Mom's the greatest because...

Cinco de Mayo!

Cinco de Mayo - May 5th!

The tiny town of Puebla, Mexico, stood prepared and ready. It was the morning of May 5, 1862, and the small Mexican army waited patiently in the forts, ready to fight.

Over six thousand French soldiers had come to take the village. As the French forces moved closer to the forts, the Mexican army opened fire. This did not stop the French. They regrouped and pushed closer until the Mexican soldiers charged on horseback and drove the French back with their swords. The Mexican cannons fired on the French. It became obvious that the mighty French soldiers, in their fancy uniforms, had been defeated by the tiny Mexican army. The Mexican army had only 2,000 men, many without weapons. The French had been too confident and thought that the taking of Puebla would be easy. They never counted on the pride and bravery of the Mexican people.

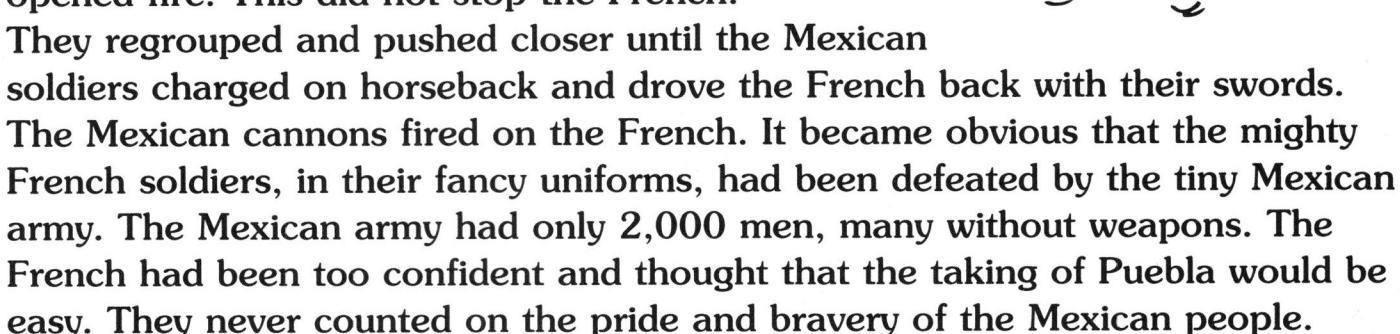

The battle of Puebla showed the world that the Mexican people would fight to keep their country and their freedom. General Zaragosa sent a report to President Benito Juarez that stated: "The Mexican army has covered itself with glory!"

Today the fifth of May, or Cinco de Mayo, is an important holiday in Mexico. It is also celebrated by Mexican-Americans here in the United States. On every Cinco de Mayo, the Mexican people stop to remember how their fathers and grandfathers fought to save the tiny town of Puebla on that great day in 1862.

ANSWER THESE QUESTIONS ABOUT CINCO DE MAYO!

1. What is the name of the town remembered on May 5th? _____
2. How many French soldiers fought the Mexican army? _____
3. What was the name of the president of Mexico? _____
4. How many men were in the Mexican army? _____
5. Why did the Mexican people fight against the French? _____
_____
6. On what day do we celebrate Cinco de Mayo? _____

Teacher's Friend Publications, Inc. ©   TF0500 May Idea Book

The Flag of Mexico

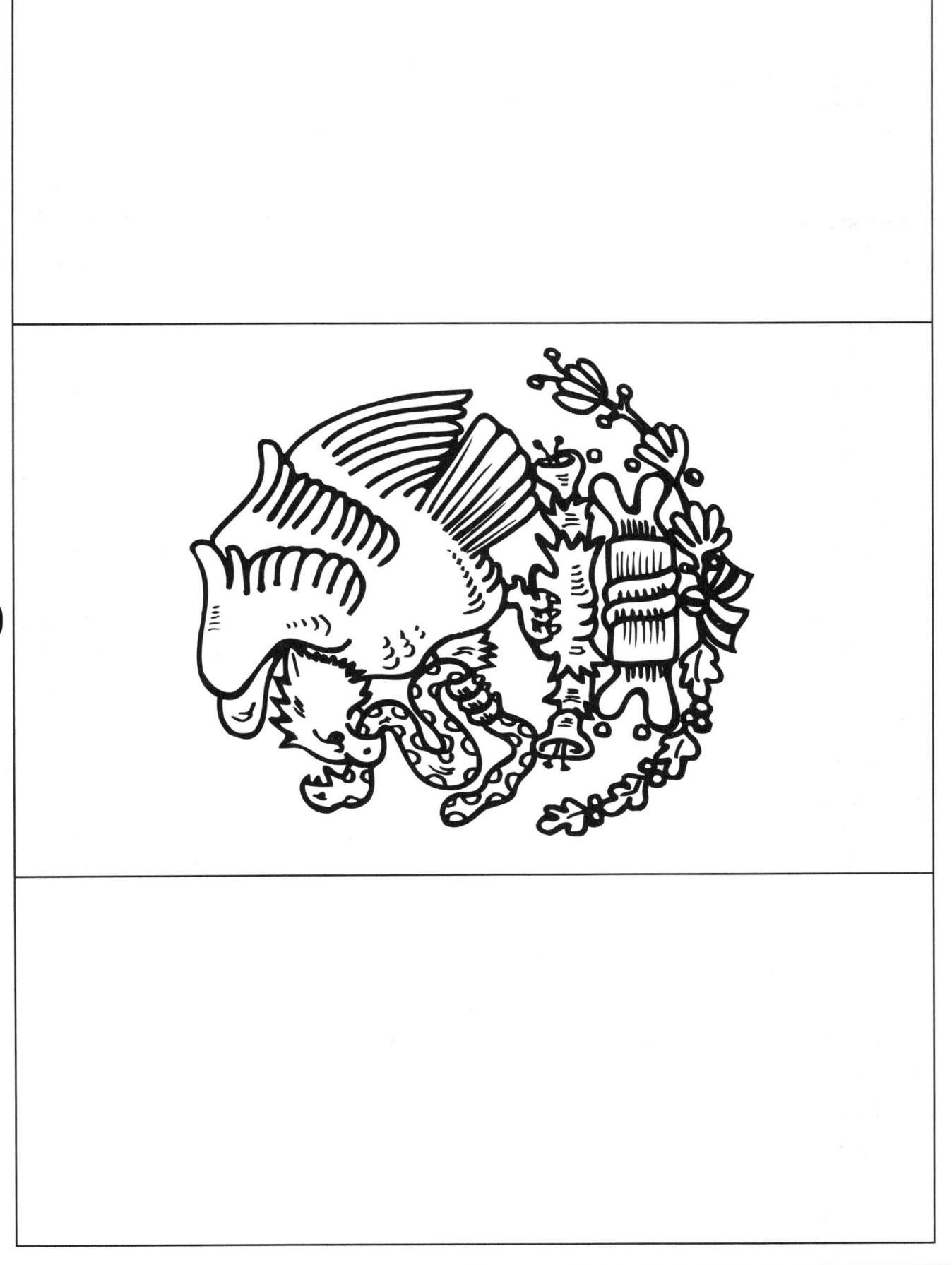

Ojo de Dios!

THE HISTORY OF OJO DE DIOS

The custom of making an Ojo de Dios is a family tradition believed to have begun with the Ruichol Indians of Mexico.

Upon the birth of a child, the father would weave a "god's eye" in the center of the two sticks. Additional rings of yarn were added each year of the child's life until his or her fifth birthday. It was believed that the Ojo de Dios was a symbol that warded off evil events. The cross formed by the two sticks symbolized the four forces of nature; earth, wind, fire and water.

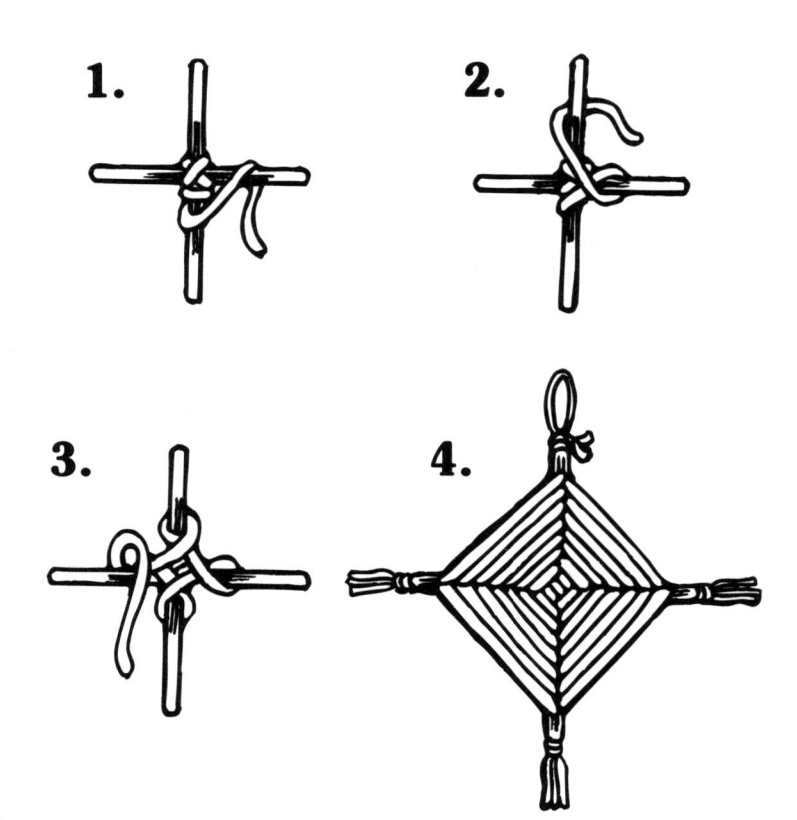

Today, the Ojo de Dios is found in the homes of many different people from various cultures. The Ojos are often considered decorations, but many families continue to display them as a symbol of home blessings. The Ojos have become an international symbol of faith and good will.

Ojo de Dios, or Eye of the Gods, are easy to make and can be used to create a colorful exhibit in your classroom.

Give each student two sticks, dowels, popsicles sticks or drinking straws. Tie the two sticks together to form a cross.

Loop the yarn around end #1 and then #2, #3, and #4, as you rotate the sticks.

Continue looping until the entire cross is full. Colors can be changed by attaching a new color of yarn to the end of the original color. Tassels can be tied to the ends of the sticks. Hang your Ojo de Dios in a window or from the class ceiling.

Cinco de Mayo Finger Puppets

Encourage students to act out a Mexican Hat Dance or the story of the Cinco de Mayo holiday with these finger puppets.

Cut Out

Cut Out

Note: Find International Children from Mexico patterns in the Teacher's Friend December Idea Book. A chapter about Mexican Independence Day is also included in the September Idea Book.

Cut Out

Cut Out

Teacher's Friend Publications, Inc. ©   TF0500 May Idea Book

The Ancient People of Mexico!

THE MAYA CIVILIZATION
The rich Maya civilization flourished over 2,000 years ago in the large southern regions of Mexico and Central America. The Maya built grand cities and huge architectural structures known as temples. They also produced beautiful paintings, pottery and sculptures. They developed an accurate yearly calendar and made great advancements in the sciences of astronomy and mathematics.

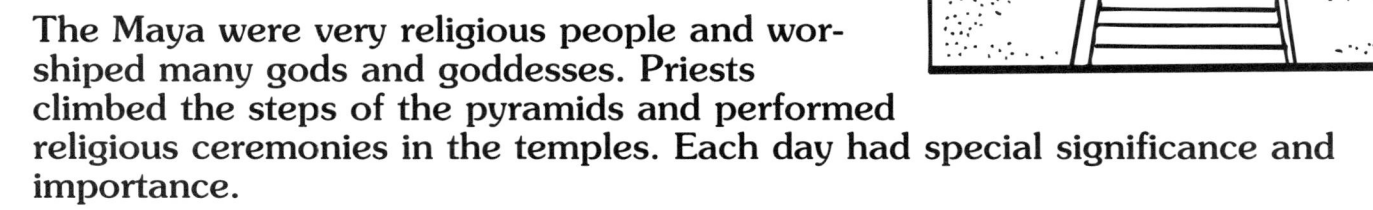

The Maya were very religious people and worshiped many gods and goddesses. Priests climbed the steps of the pyramids and performed religious ceremonies in the temples. Each day had special significance and importance.

Maya farmers grew crops of corn, beans and squash. By digging canals for irrigation, they were able to raise enough food to feed their people.

Try one of these activities with your students in their study of the Maya people:

BUILD A MAYA PYRAMID
Have your students build a Maya pyramid on the class bulletin board. Divide the class into five groups. Assign the first group as Maya Historians, the second as Maya Farmers, the third as Maya Artists, the fourth as Maya Scholars and the fifth as Maya Priests. Cut numerous 12" x 12" squares of gray construction paper and distribute one square to each student. Tell them to research information regarding their group's role in the Maya civilization and instruct them each to write a fact pertaining to their role on the gray square. (Encourage students to use additional pyramid squares.) When finished, have students pin their squares in a pyramid shape around the stair pattern you provided on the class board. Continue adding squares until the pyramid is complete.

LAND OF THE MAYA
Display a large map of Mexico and Central America on the class board. Ask students to show the areas ruled by the Maya people so long ago. Instruct them to use information from encyclopedias and locate the ancient cities and sites of Piedras Negras, Tikal, Uaxactun, Bonampak and Chichén Itza.

MAYA HIEROGLYPHICS
Have students locate in encyclopedias and resource books pictures of Maya paintings and picture writing or hieroglyphics. Ask them to create their own form of hieroglyphics and write a brief note to a friend with the pictures.

The Aztec Empire!

The American Indian people known as the Aztecs ruled the Mexican Empire over five hundred years ago. The Aztecs were an advanced civilization that ruled a large empire in central Mexico before the Spanish conquest. It was the Aztec people that founded the city of Tenochtitlan. This city was established on an island in the middle of a large lake. The Aztecs built raised earthen roads linking the island to the mainland. The site of Tenochtitlan later became the site of the capital of Mexico, Mexico City.

Under the sophisticated Aztec government leaders were chosen from a royal family and wealthy nobles had slaves that worked their land. Most slaves were captured prisoners or were bought from other groups.

The Aztecs worshiped several gods. One was Tonatiuh, the sun god. His face is in the center of the Aztec Calendar Stone. The stone is probably the most famous Aztec sculptures known to exist. The stone measures 12 feet in diameter. The other carvings on the stone are believed to represent the days of the month and symbols of the universe.

Agriculture was of extremely important in Aztec life. Corn was the largest crop, along with avocados, sweet potatoes and tomatoes. The Aztecs also produced cotton, rubber and cacao beans (chocolate).

The Spanish explorer Hernando Cortés landed on the shores of Mexico in 1519. He marched his men to the Aztec capital and overtook the city.

Try one of these activities with your students in their study of the Aztec Empire:

AZTEC DELICACIES

The Aztecs ate several foods that we continue to enjoy today. A thin cornmeal pancake called a *tlaxcalli*, in Spanish tortilla, was a daily staple to the Aztec family. They wrapped the *tlaxcallis* around bits of meat and vegetables to make *tacos*! Make tacos in the classroom or ask a parent to come in and demonstrate how to make fresh tortillas. Chocolate was a favorite drink of the Aztecs. Let your students sip a cup of cocoa while you read them a story about Aztec life.

THE AZTEC MARKET

The marketplace in Tlatelolco was probably the largest in the western hemisphere. It offered goods and merchandise of every available kind. The Aztec people would usually barter or trade for goods they needed. Arrange a marketplace in your classroom. Send a note home to parents explaining the activity and encourage them to supply items their children can trade or barter. On the given day, arrange the desks in wide rows and tell each student to display his or her "wares" on their desktops. (They may want to decorate with colorful cloths and signs explaining their merchandise.) Encourage students to negotiate with other "merchants" to trade their wares. Items left over can either be donated to a charity or returned home.

Maya Pyramid Staircase

Enlarge this staircase and have students make a Maya Pyramid on the class bulletin board.

Students may also like to make individual pyramids. Spanish vocabulary words can be written on the steps.

Teacher's Friend Publications, Inc. ©   TF0500 May Idea Book

Aztec Calendar

The Aztecs were an advanced civilization that ruled a large empire in central Mexico. They developed a very accurate calendar, much like the calendar we use today. Their calendar had 365 days in a year, just like our calendar. The Aztec calendar was divided into cycles of time. The Aztecs believed that events would repeat themselves every fifty-two years.

Teachers: Add your own math problems to the calendar. Children can color the calendar after their work is completed.

Mexican Food!

QUESADILLAS

Have each child make his or her own quesadilla in celebration of Cinco de Mayo!

Give each student a flour tortilla and two slices of American or cheddar cheese. Heat a small amount of butter in a hot skillet. Place the tortilla in the butter and place the cheese in the center. Fold the tortilla over the cheese and turn to brown the other side. Serve with hot sauce or guacamole.

(Quesadillas can be made even more simply by melting cheese-filled tortillas in a microwave oven.)

SALSA

Have students bring from home ripe tomatoes, onions, chilies and cilantro. Let them take turns cutting up the vegetables. Add a little salt and sugar. Provide a bag of tortilla chips for student dipping.

Spanish Bingo Words!

This Spanish Bingo game offers an exciting way to introduce common Spanish words to your students. Give each child a copy of the words below or write the words on the chalkboard. Ask students to write any 24 Spanish words on his or her bingo card. Use the same directions you might use for regular bingo.

After your students have mastered the Spanish words, play the bingo game again with them, writing in only the Spanish words and you giving the English interpretation.

FAMILIA - family	DOMINGO - Sunday	ROJO - rojo
PADRE - father	LUNES - Monday	AZUL - blue
MADRE - mother	MARTES - Tuesday	AMARILLO - yellow
HERMANA - sister	MIERCOLES - Wednesday	VERDE - green
HERMANO - brother	JUEVES - Thursday	BLANCO - white
TIA - aunt	VIERNES - Friday	NEGRO - black
TIO - uncle	SABADO - Saturday	UNO - one
MUCHACHA - girl	FRIO - cold	DOS - two
MUCHACHO - boy	CALIENTE - hot	TRES - three
SEÑOR - mister or man	CASA - house	CUATRO - four
SEÑORA - woman	LIBRO - book	CINCO - five
SEÑORITA - unmarried girl	MESA - table	SEIS - six
DIA - day	FIESTA - party	SIETE - seven
BUENOS DIAS - good day	SOMBRERO - hat	OCHO - eight
ADIOS - good bye	FLOR - flower	NUEVE - nine
POR FAVOR - please	BONITA - pretty	DIEZ - ten

Teacher's Friend Publications, Inc. ©

SPANISH BINGO

		FREE		

Mexican Hat Dance

The Mexican hat Dance is one of the favorite dances south of the border. Two children dance around a sombrero, shifting their weight from one foot to the other. Traditionally, the children's feet occasionally touch the wide brim of the sombrero.

Teacher's Friend Publications, Inc. ©   TF0500 May Idea Book

Our Feathered Friends!

Bird Watching Activities!

Watching and learning to identify birds can be a wonderful hobby that children can enjoy the rest of their lives. A simple walk through a park or a hike in the woods can be changed into an exciting activity by quietly observing our feathered friends.

It is important to take note of several characteristics when identifying a bird for the first time. You need to identify its shape, color, size, song and location.

Your eyes and ears are all you really need to begin bird watching, but having a pair of field glasses, or binoculars, can be a big help. You will also want to refer to a bird guidebook to assist you in identifying the birds. A small notebook can also come in handy. Write down your observations and keep a list of new birds you've discovered.

It's best to go bird watching in the early morning or just before sunset. Most birds do their feeding at this time. Move quietly or just sit and watch and listen. You'll be surprised at how many birds can be seen and enjoyed, even in your own backyard!

TRY SOME OF THESE FUN BIRD ACTIVITIES WITH YOUR STUDENTS.

CLASS BIRD BOOK
Ask children to collect pictures of various birds. Glue them into a class scrapbook and let the students write brief descriptions.

CLASS BIRD LIST
Keep an on-going list of birds found by your students. The children will love discovering new species of birds right in their own playground or backyard.

INVITE A BIRD WATCHER TO CLASS!
Ask a member of the local Audubon Society, a pet store owner or veterinarian (specializing in birds), someone who raises birds in an aviary or a great bird caller to visit your classroom!

Any of these specialists will be happy to tell about their profession or hobby and share their experiences with the class. They may even be able to bring several birds that can be observed by the students.

FEATHER FUN!
Ask students to collect a variety of feathers. Students can try to identify which feather belongs to which bird. Have students examine the feathers closely. Ask them to make special note of their color, shape, size, texture and whether of not the feather absorbs or repels water.

Bird Watching Activities!

BIRD GRAPHS
Conduct a bird feeding experiment by having students fill several bird feeders with several different types of feed. At a local feed store you will be able to find millet, sunflower seeds, suet and cracked corn. You might also like your students to try using peanut butter, peanuts, pieces of apples, raisins and bread crumbs in their feeders.

Place all of the feeders in full view of the class windows and ask students to record which feeders attract the most birds. They could also note what time of day the birds are most active and which feed disappears the quickest.

You may want to assign each feeder to a small group of students. Have the students record their findings on a graph.

EAT LIKE A BIRD MATH
A commonly used phrase for people that are small eaters is "eats like a bird!" Well, let's hope that no one in your class eats that much!

Most baby birds eat twice their weight every day! Think how much each of your students would have to eat to eat twice their weight! Have each student figure out how many quarter pound hamburgers they would have to consume before they "ate like a bird!"

BIRD QUESTIONS!
Ask your students to find out these interesting facts about birds!

What bird is the largest?
What bird is the smallest?
What bird flies the fastest?
How high do birds fly?
How many birds are there?
Can birds fly backwards?
Do all birds have nests?
How do birds get their names?

Students may like to research a few particular birds such as the ostrich or hummingbird.

A VISIT TO THE PARK
Arrange for your class to visit a local park where they can see ducks and geese up close.

Before going to the park, discuss with your students whether ducks and wild animals should be fed by humans. What happens to ducks that become dependent on the food humans give them? Will birds that normally migrate during the spring and autumn stay behind? Discuss the consequences of feeding any wild animal or bird. Students may like to list the pros and cons.

You might also want to talk about how ducks and geese in city parks are affected by pollution and other environmental hazards.

Invite a park ranger or naturalist to speak to your class before visiting the park.

Bird Feeders!

One way to attract birds is to feed them! Make one of these bird feeders and hang it outside your classroom window. The children will love to watch the many varieties of birds that come to the feeder.

BREADSTICKS AND BAGELS
Smear peanut butter on stale breadsticks or bagels and roll them in bird seed. Hang the treats on a string from a secluded tree branch.

CEREAL LOOPS
String doughnut-shaped cereal on lengths of yarn or string. Hang them from a branch outside your classroom window.

FRUIT ON A STICK
Find a sturdy stick about ten inches long and push it through an apple or pear half. Tie a string to either end of the stick and loop it over a tree branch. Birds will perch on the stick and nibble away at the fruit. (Stale doughnuts can also be used in place of tfruit.)

PLASTIC JUG FEEDER
Nearly any large plastic jug can be used to make this feeder. Cut out a large section of the jug with scissors, as shown in the illustration. Poke a hole on both sides of the jug with scissors and push a sturdy twig through the holes for the birds to use as a perch. Fill the bottom of the jug with bird seed or dry cereal. Tie a string to the neck of the jug and either hang in a tree or hammer a nail or two through the back of the jug to a fence post.

HANGING BIRD BATH
A large plastic trash can lid makes an excellent bird bath. Poke four or five evenly spaced holes around the outside edge of the lid. Tie heavy nylon twine through the holes and secure to a sturdy tree branch. Fill the lid with an inch of water and watch your feathered friends enjoy a cool bath on a hot day.

Bird Feeders!

MILK CARTON FEEDER

Staple together the top of a clean, dry milk carton. With a pair of scissors, cut out one side of the carton, leaving at least a 1/2 inch border on all four sides.

Cut a slit lengthwise from a short piece of a plastic drinking straw. Slip the straw over the bottom ridge of your opening for a perch.

Cut a small opening in the top of the carton and insert a heavy string or wire. Fill the feeder with wild birdseed and hang it in a nearby tree.

See if you can name the many different types of birds that come to feed!

FRUIT BASKET FEEDER

Cut an orange or grapefruit in half and hollow out the inside. Insert three pipe cleaners evenly around the edge of each fruit half. Bend the ends back to secure the fruit. Twist the other three ends together. Fill the "fruit basket" with birdseed and hang it by a piece of yarn in a secluded place.

One of the best things about this craft is that you get to eat the orange or grapefruit!

HUMMINGBIRD FEEDER

Ask your students to bring to class a clean, plastic bottle. Heat an ice pick and make several evenly spaced holes around the bottle, about three inches from the bottom. Attach a wire to the top for hanging. Fill the feeder with hummingbird food, making sure that the level of the liquid is not above the holes. Hang the feeder in a tree, out of reach of other animals. It will be fun to watch the hummingbirds feed this spring and summer!

Hummingbird Food
    1/2 cup sugar
    1/2 cup water
    Several drops of red
        food coloring

Boil the mixture and let it cool before filling the feeder.

BIRDS OF A FEATHER

Ask your students to bring in feathers from various birds that they have found. Assist them in identifying the birds to which the feathers might belong. Have the children examine the feathers. Ask them to draw a picture of the feathers, noting their texture, shape and color. Have the children sprinkle water on the feathers to see if they absorb or repel water.

Teacher's Friend Publications, Inc. ©   TF0500 May Idea Book

Bird Paper Bag Puppet

Cut this bird puppet pattern from construction paper. Glue the head and the body to a small brown paper lunch bag. Staple both wings to either side of the bag.

Children will have fun flying their birds around the classroom!

Cut 2 wings

85

Teacher's Friend Publications, Inc. ©   TF0500 May Idea Book

Duck Tales

Display students' good work papers or creative duck tales with this "ducky" idea!

Cut the two duck patterns from white construction paper. Color its beak orange. Arrange the pattern pieces on each side of a child's paper, as shown. Title your display "We Keep Our Ducks In A Row!", or "Ducky Papers!"

Teacher's Friend Publications, Inc. ©   TF0500 May Idea Book

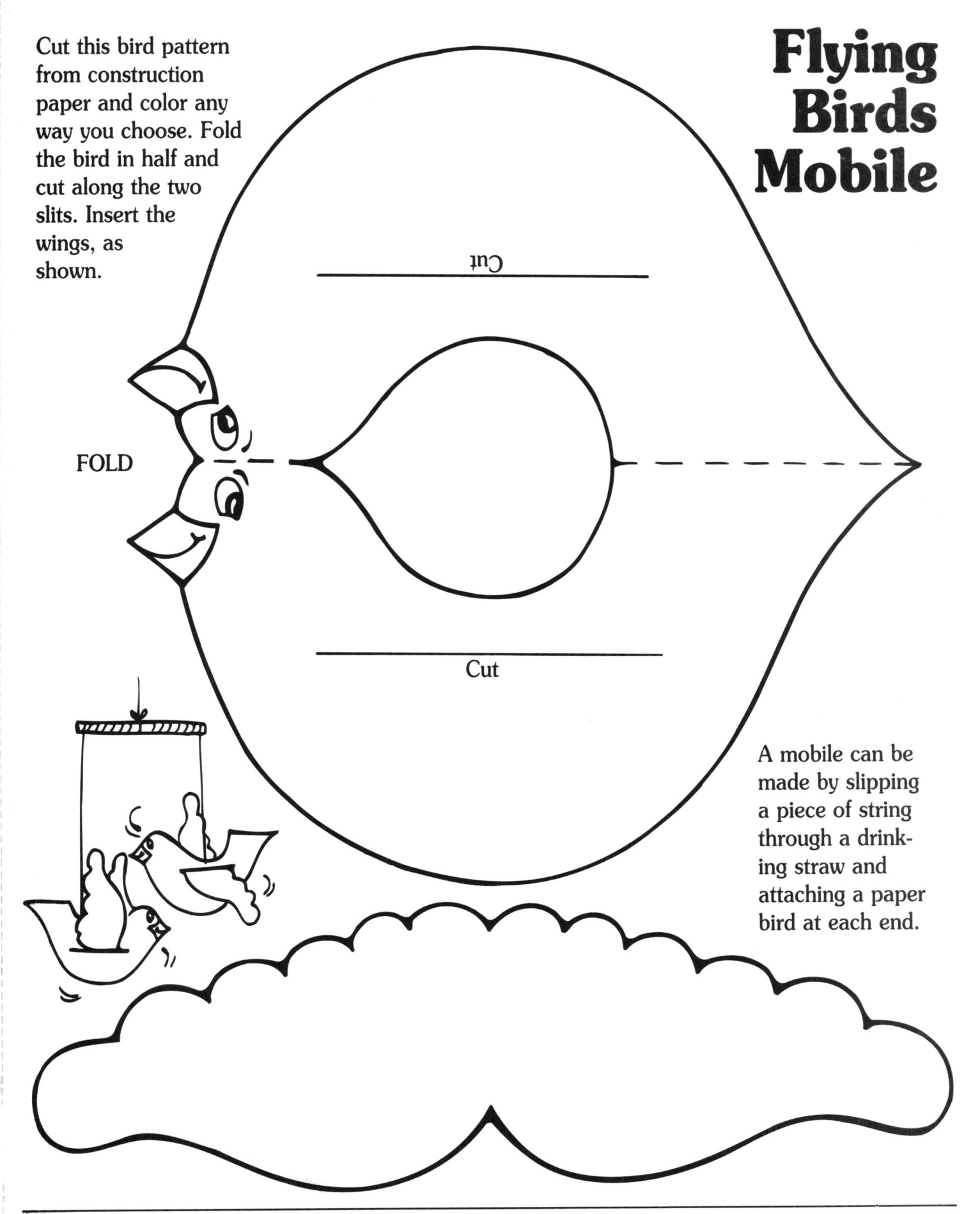

Cut this bird pattern from construction paper and color any way you choose. Fold the bird in half and cut along the two slits. Insert the wings, as shown.

Flying Birds Mobile

Cut

FOLD

Cut

A mobile can be made by slipping a piece of string through a drinking straw and attaching a paper bird at each end.

Teacher's Friend Publications, Inc. ©

TF0500 May Idea Book

Help Mother Bird Find Her Nest!

4. 5. 6. 7. 8. 9. 10. 11. 12. 13. 14.

28. 29. 30.

TEACHERS: Two, three or four children can play this game. Make your own task cards or write math problems that must be solved in each square.

Parts of a Bird

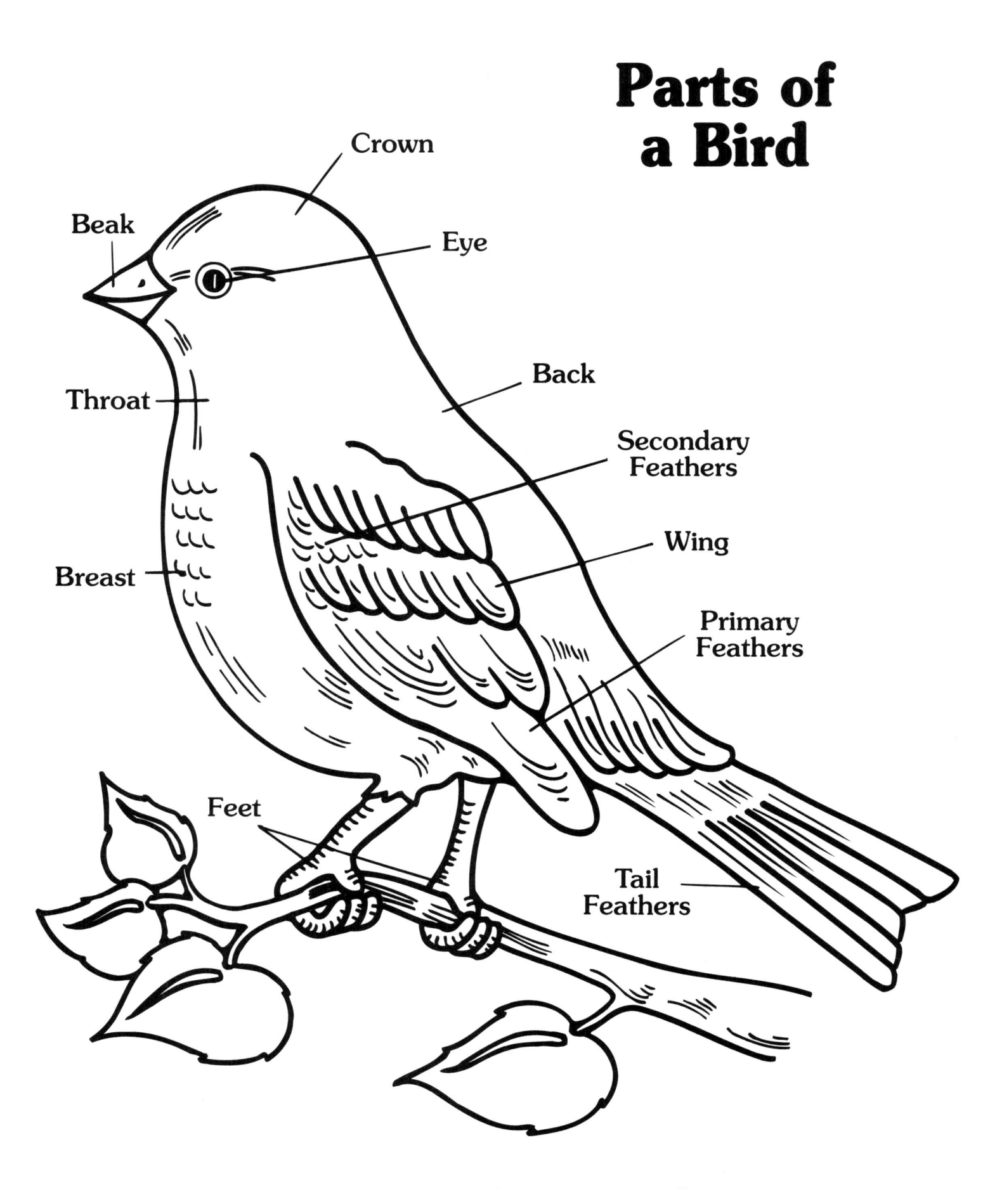

- Crown
- Beak
- Eye
- Throat
- Back
- Secondary Feathers
- Wing
- Breast
- Primary Feathers
- Feet
- Tail Feathers

MY BIRD WATCHING BOOK!

_____
Name

Bird Watching

Bird watching can be a lot of fun, especially if you know what to look for!

When looking for birds, move very slowly and quietly, keeping your eyes and ears open.

When you see a bird, stand very still and watch closely without making any sudden movements. Use field glasses, if you have them.

Try to identify the bird using these guidelines:

- **LOCATION**
- **SIZE**
- **SHAPE**
- **COLOR**
- **SONG or CALL**

Record your bird watching adventure!

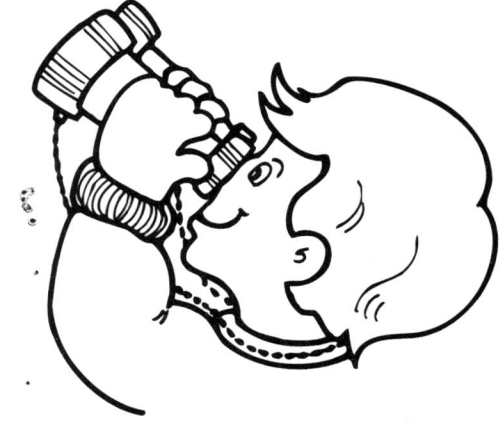

Date: _____

Time: _____

Place: _____

_____

Weather Conditions: _____

_____

Bird Watching!

LOCATION:
Some birds are found at the seashore, while others prefer open fields or wooded areas.

In the city, you will find most birds in parks or on playgrounds though many also like to build their homes under the eaves of tall buildings.

Where did you find your bird?

- ☐ Lake
- ☐ Woods
- ☐ Seashore
- ☐ Field
- ☐ Park
- ☐ Backyard
- ☐ Playground
- ☐ Other

Describe the location where you found your bird: _____
_____
_____

What was your bird doing? _____
_____

Did you see your bird's nest? _____
Describe it: _____
_____
_____

Teacher's Friend Publications, Inc. © TF0500 May Idea Book

Bird Watching!

SIZE:
The best way to determine the size of a bird is to compare its size to the size of a bird you know.

A pigeon might be a good example to use.

Compared to a pigeon, is your bird:

- ☐ Much larger
- ☐ A little larger
- ☐ Much smaller
- ☐ A little smaller
- ☐ About the same size

Here is a picture of a pigeon.

Draw a picture of your bird comparing its size to that of a pigeon.

Bird Watching!

SHAPE:
Next, identify your bird by it's shape.

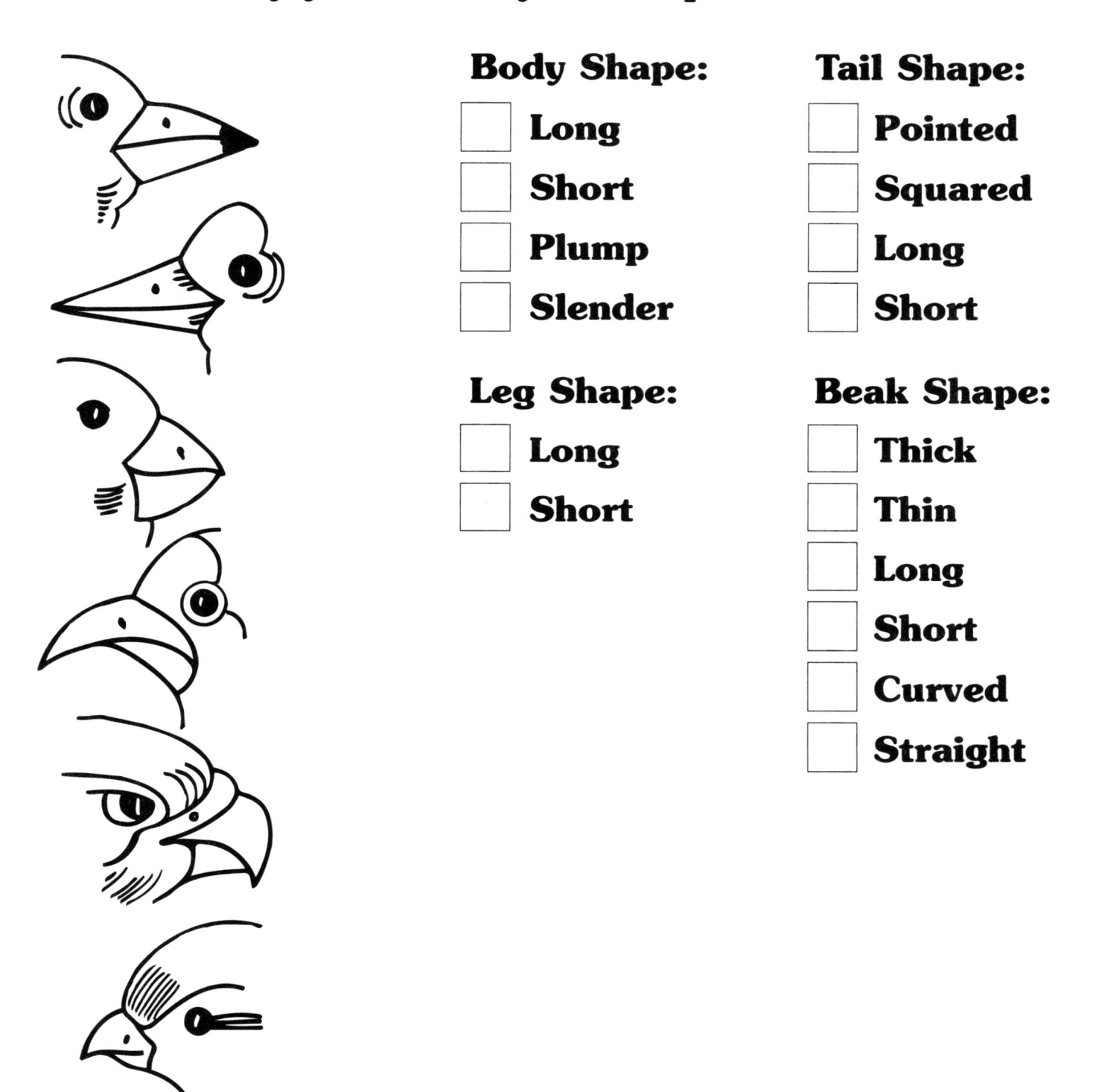

Body Shape:
- [ ] Long
- [ ] Short
- [ ] Plump
- [ ] Slender

Tail Shape:
- [ ] Pointed
- [ ] Squared
- [ ] Long
- [ ] Short

Leg Shape:
- [ ] Long
- [ ] Short

Beak Shape:
- [ ] Thick
- [ ] Thin
- [ ] Long
- [ ] Short
- [ ] Curved
- [ ] Straight

Draw a picture of your bird showing the shape of its body, tail, legs and beak.

Bird Watching!

COLOR:
What color is your bird? Determine the color of your bird's....

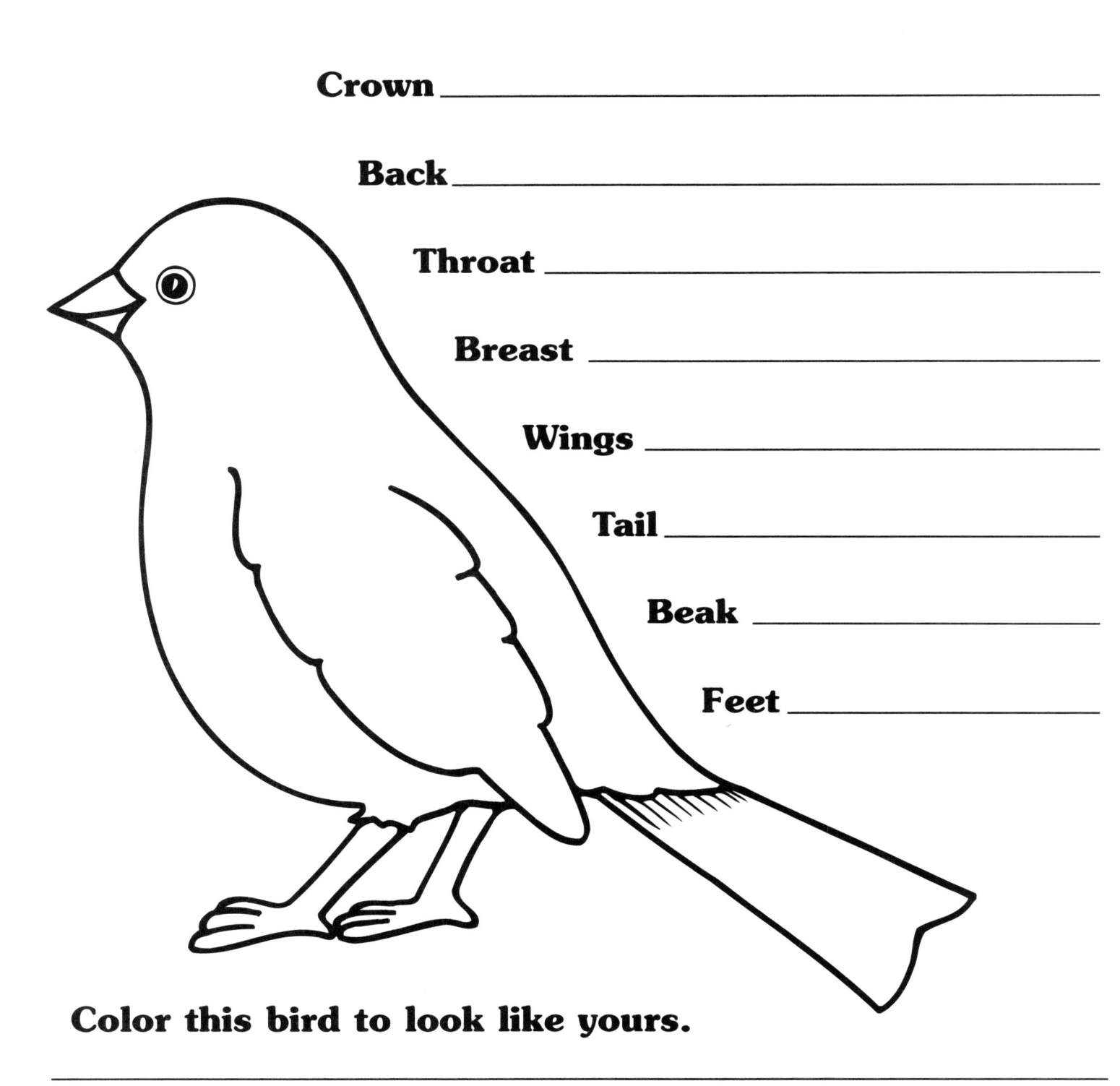

Crown _____

Back _____

Throat _____

Breast _____

Wings _____

Tail _____

Beak _____

Feet _____

Color this bird to look like yours.

Bird Watching!

SONG or CALL:
Listen to the sound your bird makes.

Some birds, like a chickadee, say their names. Others have squeaks, chirps or squawks. Many sing beautiful tunes.

Can you imitate your bird's sound?

Describe yous bird's song or call.

_____
_____
_____
_____
_____

Teacher's Friend Publications, Inc. ©   TF0500 May Idea Book

Bird Watching!

I've identified my bird! It is a...

_____

This is what I've learned about my bird!

_____
_____
_____
_____
_____
_____
_____
_____
_____

Report completed on: _____

Duckling Pattern!

Create a duck pond scene on your class bulletin board. Make several duckling patterns from yellow construction paper and label them with alphabet letters, ordinal numbers, dictionary words, etc. Ask students to arrange the ducklings in order. Label the board, "We've Got Our Ducks in a Row!"

Bird Names!

ACTIVITY 1   FIND THESE BIRD NAMES IN THE PUZZLE BELOW.

YELLOWHAMMER
PTARMIGAN
WREN
MOCKINGBIRD
QUAIL
BUNTING
ROBIN
CHICKEN
THRASHER
GOOSE
BLUEBIRD
CARDINAL
GOLDFINCH
MEADOWLARK
PELICAN
CHICKADEE
ORIOLE
LOON
FINCH
ROADRUNNER
FLYCATCHER
GROUSE
PHEASANT
GULL
THRUSHER

```
Z C V G T Y H N F L Y C A T C H E R E V C
Q W C V G T B G I J K L O P U Y T R E W D
U C H I C K E N N F R T Y H J K I L O O N
A D F G T G B H C E R T Y W R E N F T G H
I D F U R T G C H I C K A D E E V B G H Y
L E R L Y E L L O W H A M M E R R W E C S
V E R L D R E T F G T H B T F O G O O S E
B L U E B I R D D R T G B Y H B W Q X W T
V G H Y U J O R I O L E E D R I D C V B G
P E R G D R P T A R M I G A N N E R T Y U
E W Q R C A R D I N A L P H E A S A N T Y
L D R T G F V B N H J U K I O L P M G R T
I T H R U S H E R E R T F G B U N T I N G
C D R E F G T Y H M O C K I N G B I R D Q
A R T Y U I D F V G B N H J K M U Y R E W
N D E R O A D R U N N E R E W Q S D T Y U
G R O U S E G O L D F I N C H W Q E T Y O
X V M E A D O W L A R K F G E F G V B H J
T H R A S H E R E W Q V B N M K J S W R T
```

Teacher's Friend Publications, Inc. ©   99   TF0500 May Idea Book

Bird Sequence Cards

Teacher's Friend Publications, Inc. ©   100   TF0500 May Idea Book

The Big Top!

Circus Activities!

As the close of school approaches, motivate your students to continue their learning progress with these exciting, circus activities!

CLASS CIRCUS BOOK

Assign each student a letter of the alphabet. Children must select an animal or circus attraction that begins with that letter and illustrate their selection on a sheet of paper. The papers are then stapled together in alphabetical order and labeled "Our Class Circus Book!"

You may need to label the top of each paper for younger children. Examples include:

"A" is for Acrobat
"B" is for Bears
"C" is for Clown
"D" is for Daredevil
"E" is for Elephant

CLOWN COLLEGE

Did you know that there is really a Clown College? One or more of your students may want to request information on a clowning career. Have them write to: Clown College, Ringling Bros., Barnum and Bailey Circus, P.O. Box 1528, Venice, Florida 34284.

Ringling Bros., Barnum and Bailey Circus also offers some free teaching materials about the circus. To receive information and a newsletter, write to: Department of Educational Services, Ringling Bros., Barnum and Bailey Circus, 8607 Westwood Center Drive, Vienna, VA 22182.

HOW BIG IS AN ELEPHANT?

On the school playground, have students draw a life-size elephant using chalk.

African male elephants stand as tall as 10 feet at the shoulders and weigh as much as 6 tons. Their ears can be as large as 4 feet wide and their tusks 8 feet long. Have students use a yardstick to measure the dimensions of their elephants.

Children might also like to know that an elephant eats about 250 pounds of plants and drinks 50 gallons of water every day. Ask students to figure how many cartons of milk would equal 50 gallons and to estimate the number of hamburgers it would take to total 250 pounds.

PEANUT MATH

Everyone knows that elephants love peanuts, so why not let this nutritious treat motivate your students with some math activities?

Give each student a handful of shelled peanuts. Introduce simple math problems by having students arrange the peanuts in groups. For example, children can easily see that three groups of five peanuts is exactly the same as five groups of three peanuts.

Ask students to practice estimation by guessing the number of peanuts in a jar or bag. Have the students count the peanuts and see who came the closest. (You may want the children to count by twos, threes or fives.)

Of course, children can eat these math manipulatives when the activity is completed.

Circus Activities!

CIRCUS PANTOMIMES
Young children will love this activity! Give each student the name of a circus performer or animal to act out. Children take turns imitating the various performers or animals. Classmates can guess the appropriate name or profession.

CIRCUS HISTORY
Children will enjoy finding library and resource books that tell about the origin of the modern day circus. Students may like to make a "Circus Timeline" showing when different attractions were first shown. You might also like to add important dates to see how social and political events have affected circus life.

Make sure that your students include such circus greats as General Tom Thumb, Jumbo the Elephant, Joseph Grimaldi, Emmett Kelley, Jenny Lind, The Wallendas and P.T. Barnum, James Bailey and the Ringling Brothers.

CIRCUS HISTORY
Did your students know that circus animals come from all over the world? Have them research various circus animals. For instance, they will find that in India only male elephants have tusks, while in Africa, both males and females have them. Students may like to make a chart on the chalkboard noting the names of different circus animals and their country of origin. Ask them to then find the individual countries on the classroom map or globe.

CIRCUS VOCABULARY
Nearly all specialized occupations have developed their own vocabulary. The circus is no exception. Here are some of the unusual words still used in the circus today.

- Annie Oakley - free pass or ticket
- Back Lot - rear entrance where animals are kept
- Ballyhoo - to attract attention
- Big Bertha - Ringling Bros., Barnum and Bailey Circus
- Blues - general admission seats
- Boss Hostler - one in charge of horses
- Bulls - elephants (males and females)
- Cats - lions, tigers, leopards, panthers
- Cherry Pie - extra work for extra pay
- Clown Alley - clowns' dressing room
- Dog and Pony Show - small circus
- Donikers - rest rooms
- Fliers - aerialists
- Finale - when all performers take their last bow
- Hippodrome - track between the seats and performing rings.
- Howdah - chair carried on the back of an animal, usually an elephant
- Joey - a clown
- Jump - distance from city to city
- Kinker - any circus performer
- Midway - area in front of the main entrance
- Ray - tent
- Red Wagon - main office of the circus
- Shekles - money
- Tail-up - command to an elephant to follow in line
- Trunk-up - command to an elephant to raise his trunk in salute
- Turnaway - a sell-out

Circus Finger Puppets

Cut Out · Cut Out
Cut Out · Cut Out
Cut Out · Cut Out
Cut Out

Teacher's Friend Publications, Inc. © 104 TF0500 May Idea Book

Movable Clown

Cut this clown from colored paper and assemble with brass fasteners.

Three-Ring Circus!

Create a "Three-Ring Circus" in your classroom with these fun-filled activities. You might like to ask the children to come dressed as their favorite circus character for the day.

Begin your circus adventure by playing circus music or one of John Philip Sousa's inspirational tunes. Announce to your class that the circus has begun. Try something like this:

> "Ladies and gentlemen, boy and girls, the _____ School, right here in room_____, proudly announces the arrival of the greatest show on earth! Kindly focus your attention to the center ring where contestants from around the world will perform death-defying feats in the art of spelling and mathematics! And now, what you've all been waiting for, the CIRCUS! Let the show begin!!!"

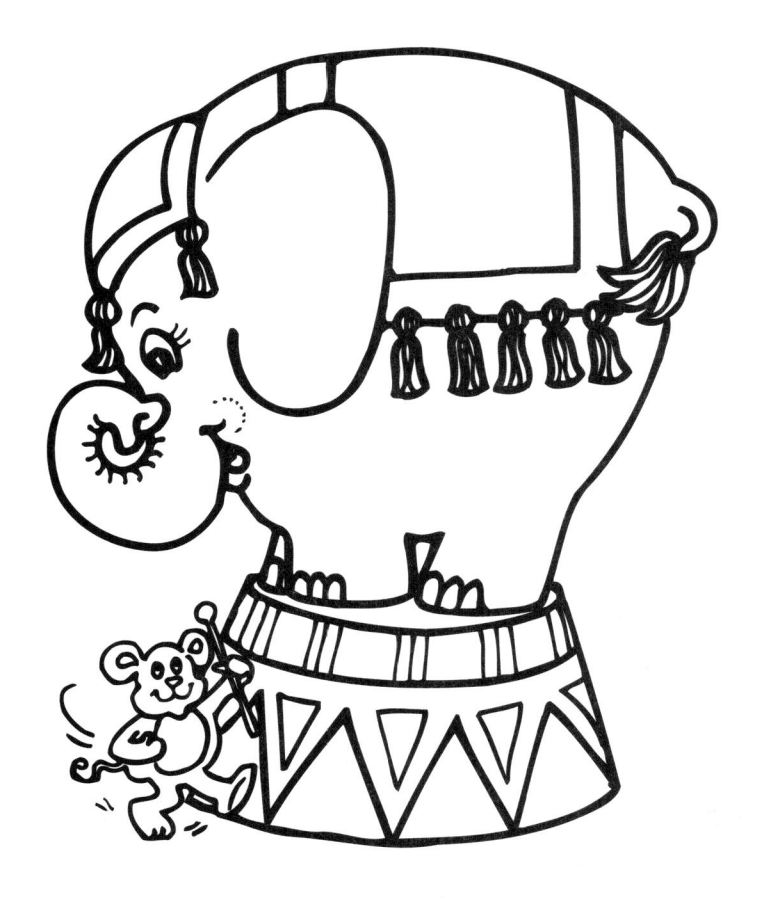

RING #1

The "clowns" in your class will love the spotlight and attention they receive while participating in this math activity.

Write a variety of funny consequences on strips of colored paper, such as "Make a funny face!" or "Do ten jumping jacks!"

Select four or five "clowns" to perform for the class. Give each one a math problem to solve verbally. If they fail to answer correctly, they must choose a consequence to perform in front of their classmates. Keep score of the results and award the "clown" with the most correct answers with a balloon!

Three Ring Circus!

RING #2

Your most competent spellers will be eager to walk the "highwire" with this fun activity.

Place a balance beam or long strip of tape across the classroom floor. "Tightrope walkers" carefully walk the "highwire," balancing with a broomstick or yardstick, while spelling words given by the ringmaster. Slips on the "wire" are not counted against the performer, only misspelled words. The "tightrope walker" with the most successfully spelled words wins a prize.

RING #3

Select a "lion tamer" to stand in a circle of ten or twelve "lions."

Each "lion" takes a turn giving the tamer a multiplication problem to be solved. If the tamer answers correctly, he/she remains in the center of the circle. If the tamer answers incorrectly, the lion can give the correct answer and then take the tamer's place in the circle. Each "lion" must try to become the "lion tamer" for the longest period of time.

Award all of the lions and tamers with small bags of popcorn at the end of the performance.

Make sure you include everyone in your three-ring circus. As the head ringmaster, be certain to coach the audience to "ooh" and "aah" at the appropriate times. Other circus acts such as a beanbag toss or team relay races, can also be included.

Peanut Pattern

Elephant Paper Bag Puppet

Cut these elephant puppet patterns from gray construction paper. Glue both patterns to a small paper lunch bag.

109

Elephant Mask

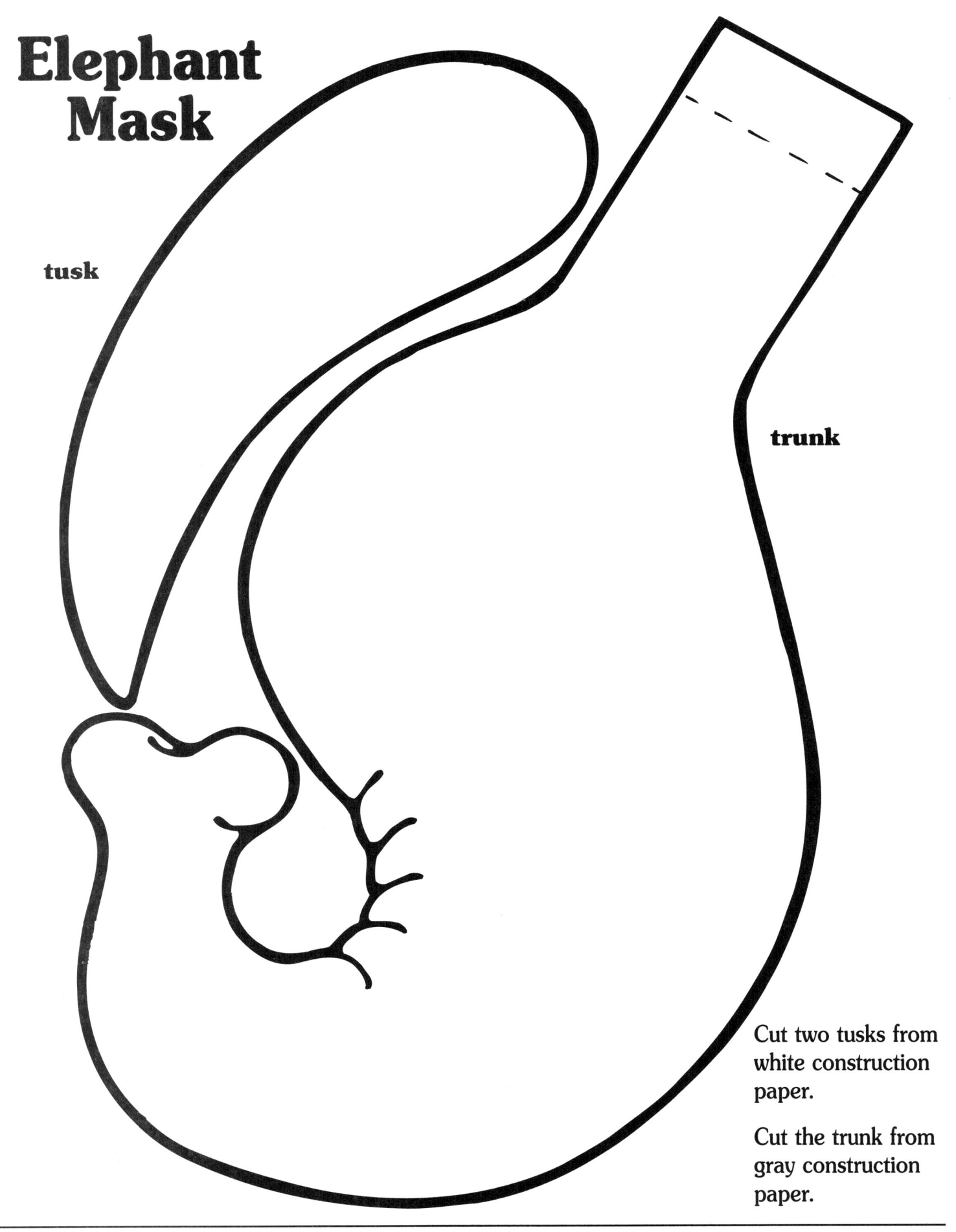

tusk

trunk

Cut two tusks from white construction paper.

Cut the trunk from gray construction paper.

Teacher's Friend Publications, Inc. ©   110   TF0500 May Idea Book

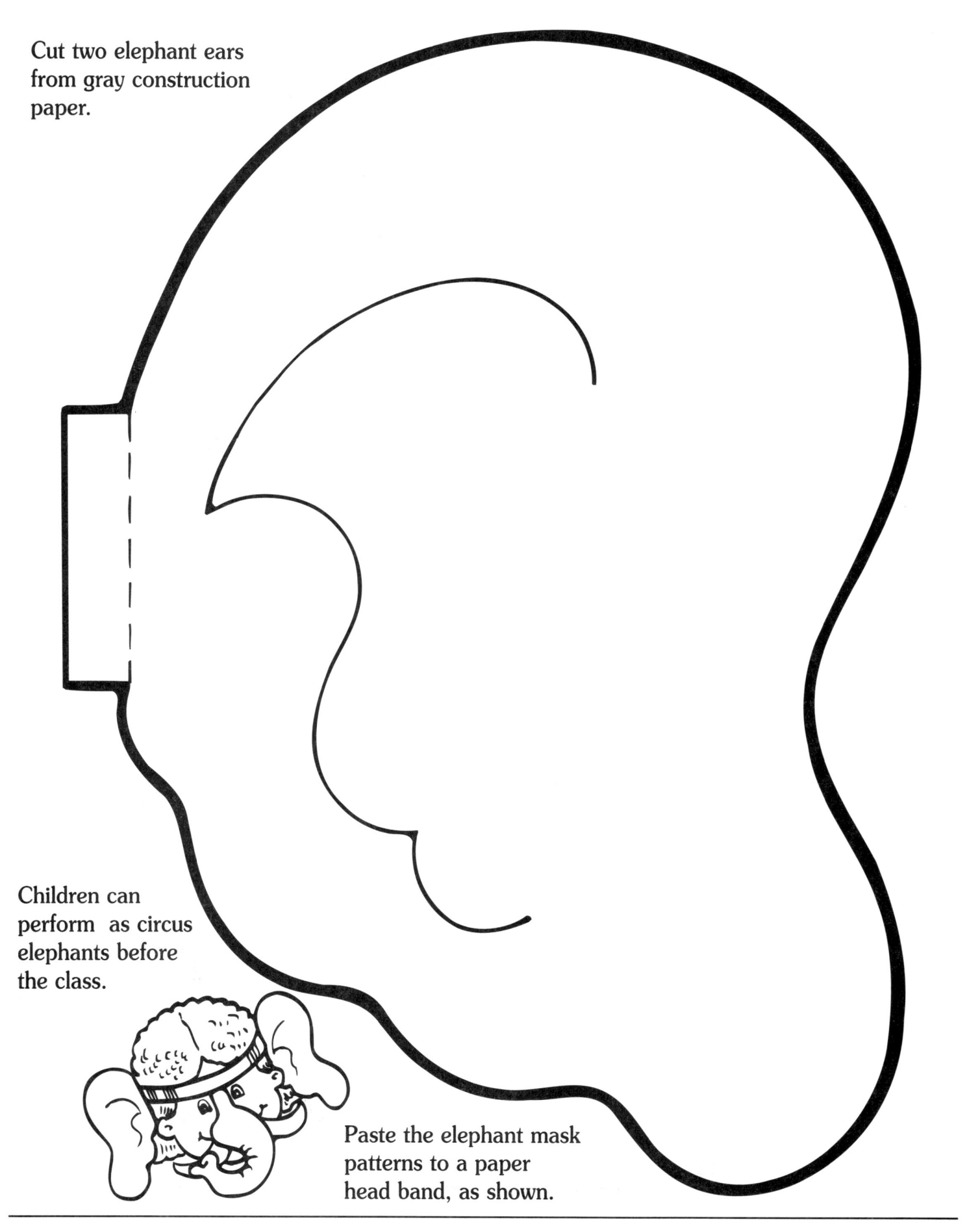

Cut two elephant ears from gray construction paper.

Children can perform as circus elephants before the class.

Paste the elephant mask patterns to a paper head band, as shown.

Teacher's Friend Publications, Inc. © 111 TF0500 May Idea Book

Circus Word Find!

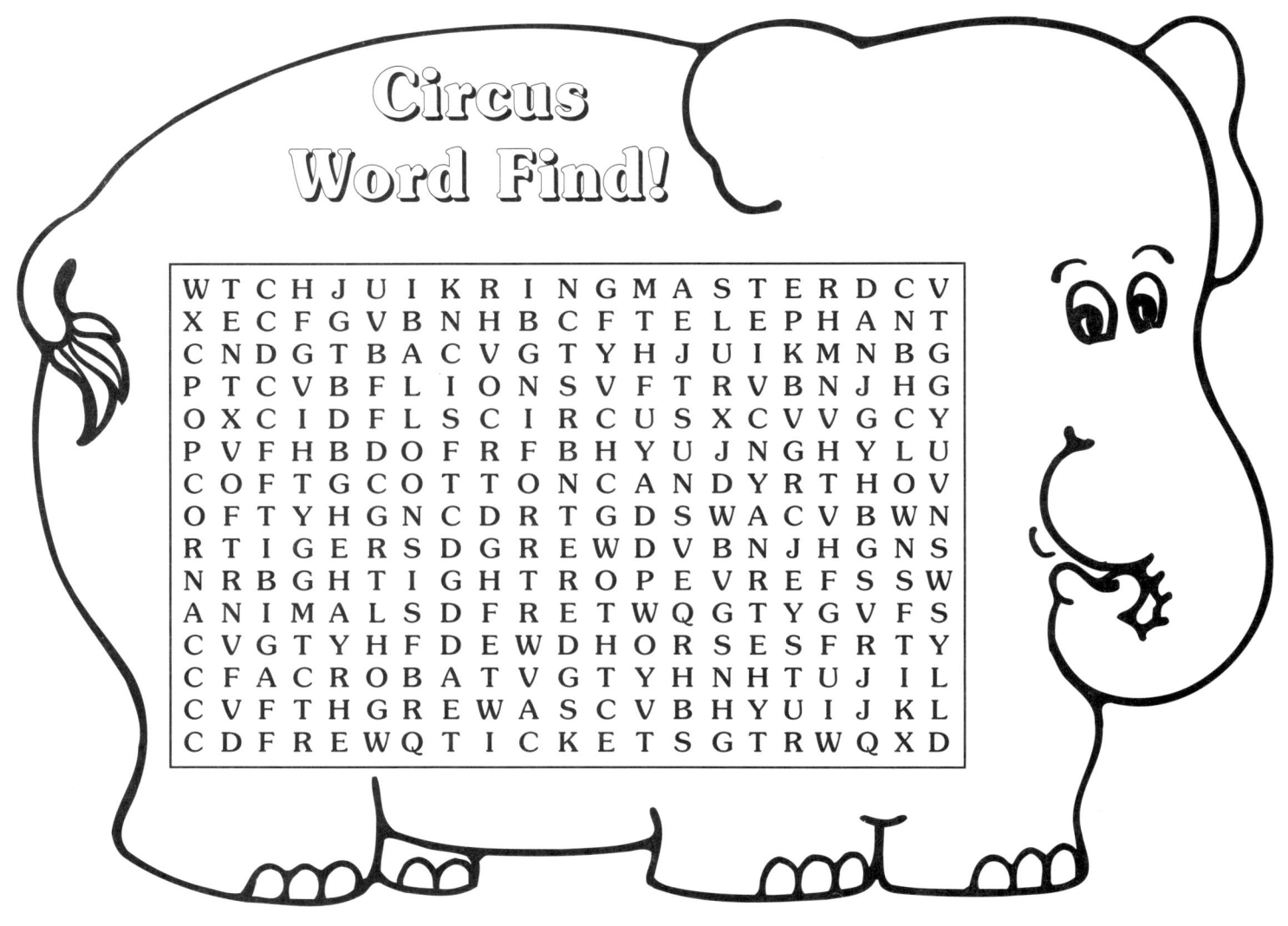

```
W T C H J U I K R I N G M A S T E R D C V
X E C F G V B N H B C F T E L E P H A N T
C N D G T B A C V G T Y H J U I K M N B G
P T C V B F L I O N S V F T R V B N J H G
O X C I D F L S C I R C U S X C V V G C Y
P V F H B D O F R F B H Y U J N G H Y L U
C O F T G C O T T O N C A N D Y R T H O V
O F T Y H G N C D R T G D S W A C V B W N
R T I G E R S D G R E W D V B N J H G N S
N R B G H T I G H T R O P E V R E F S S W
A N I M A L S D F R E T W Q G T Y G V F S
C V G T Y H F D E W D H O R S E S F R T Y
C F A C R O B A T V G T Y H N H T U J I L
C V F T H G R E W A S C V B H Y U I J K L
C D F R E W Q T I C K E T S G T R W Q X D
```

ACTIVITY 2

FIND THESE CIRCUS WORDS IN THE PUZZLE: TIGHTROPE, COTTON CANDY, TENT, ACROBAT, TICKETS, CIRCUS, RINGMASTER, ANIMALS, CLOWNS, ELEPHANT, BALLOONS, TIGERS, POPCORN, LIONS, HORSES

Write a paragraph about the circus using at least six words from the Word Find Puzzle.

_____

_____

_____

_____

_____

Teacher's Friend Publications, Inc. ©   TF0500 May Idea Book

Stand-Up Circus Animals

FOLD

FOLD

Copy these animal patterns onto heavy paper. Fold, cut out and color. Stand the animals on a desk top.

Create a Clown Face!

Create your own clown face by using the various mouth, eyebrows and nose patterns on the next page.

Cut out the clown face and paste it onto a separate sheet of heavy paper. Draw in the clown's hair and color his/her hat and collar.

Teacher's Friend Publications, Inc. ©   TF0500 May Idea Book

Mouths

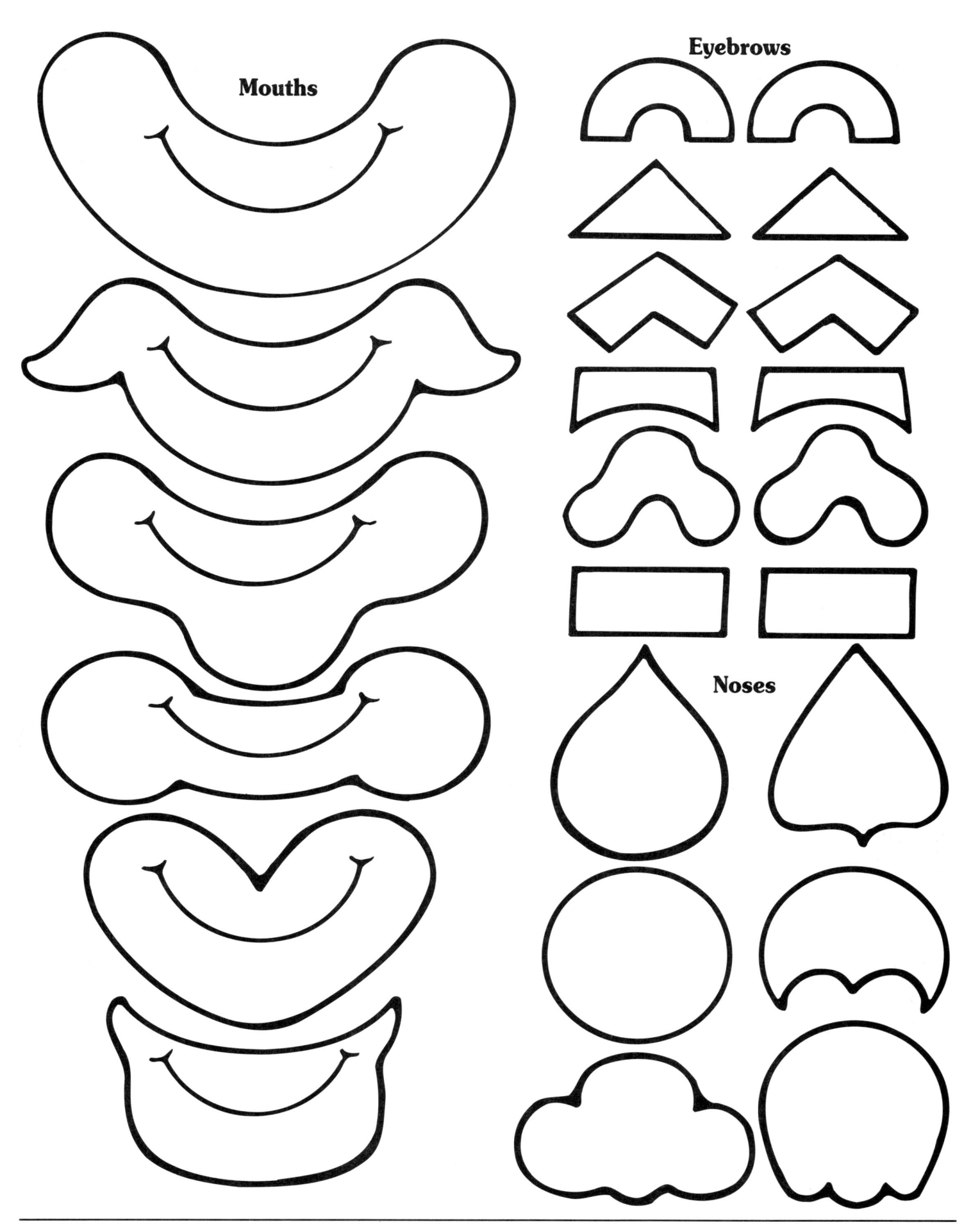

Eyebrows

Noses

Teacher's Friend Publications, Inc. ©   115   TF0500 May Idea Book

Clown Wheel

Copy this "Clown Wheel" onto heavy index paper. Color, cut out and assemble with brass fasteners. Cut out the two boxes, as shown.

Cut Out

Cut Out

Teacher's Friend Publications, Inc. © TF0500 May Idea Book

Add your own math problems or word contractions to the wheel.

Move the ice cream cone to reveal the correct answer.

Make a "Clown Wheel" for each child in class.

Teacher's Friend Publications, Inc. © 117 TF0500 May Idea Book

Mr. Clown

Cut these pattern pieces from heavy paper and color with crayons. Paste the patterns around a sheet of construction paper mounted with a student's good work paper.

My Circus Report

_____
Student's Name

I've learned three important things about the circus. They are:

1. _____
   _____

2. _____
   _____

3. _____

_____

My favorite circus act is _____
_____

My favorite circus animal is a _____
_____

If I were a circus performer, I'd like to be _____
_____

because _____
_____
_____

My favorite thing to eat at the circus is _____
_____

If I owned a circus, I'd call it _____
_____
_____

Teacher's Friend Publications, Inc. ©   TF0500 May Idea Book

Clown Color Page

Teachers: Add your own math problems to this clown character. Instruct students to solve the problems before coloring.

Teacher's Friend Publications, Inc. © 120 TF0500 May Idea Book

FOLD

My Circus Book

Name

Teacher's Friend Publications, Inc. ©   121   TF0500 May Idea Book

Circus Writing

Zoo Animals!

Zoo Animal Activities!

Use the theme of zoo animals to encourage your students' vocabulary and research skills. Try some of these fun activities:

ZOO FIELD TRIP
Arrange a field trip to the local zoo. Make sure that students have made a list of the animals they wish to see the day before you go. (A list and description of various types of monkeys may come in handy.)

If a field trip is not possible, ask a zoo representative or exotic pet shop owner to visit your classroom. They may be able to bring a small monkey or other animal along!

ANIMAL QUESTIONS
After your students have discovered the unique qualities of many of the world's animals, ask them to answer the following questions.

Name an animal that....

....doesn't eat meat.
....is endangered.
... is a fast runner.
....does work for people.
....has a pouch.
....makes an unusual sound.
....has been trapped for its fur.
....migrates.
....is an herbivore.
....protects itself in a special way.
....can blend into its surroundings.
....has tusks.
....is born from an egg.
....can walk right after its born.
....has claws.
....sleeps most of the day.
....doesn't have hair.
....spends most of its time in the water.

YES OR NO ANIMALS
Your students can practice their knowledge about animals with this fun game.

Pin a picture or name of an animal on each child's back. (Make sure they don't see it.) The students then ask other students yes and no questions relating to their animal. Some questions might be "Do I have stripes?" "Do I live in a rainforest?" "Can I fly?"

When the children guess their animals correctly, they may take the picture and pin it to the front of their shirts.

I'M GOING TO THE ZOO
Have your students practice both their alphabetical and memorization skills with this simple game.

Tell the students to sit in a circle. Assign one student to start by saying, "I'm going to the zoo and I'm going to see an Aardvark!" The student's response should begin with the first letter of the alphabet, "A". The next student repeats what the previous student said and adds his or her response, beginning with the letter "B". For example, "I'm going to the zoo and I'm going to see an Aardvark and a Baboon!" The game continues around the circle. (Not all responses need to be animals.) If students fail to remember or use a wrong letter, they lose their turn and must sit in the center of the circle.

Zoo Animal Activities!

ENDANGERED ANIMALS
Your students might like to join an organization with the purpose of saving and protecting endangered wildlife. Have them write to:

The Jane Goodall Institute of Wildlife Research, Education and Conservation
1601 W. Anklam Road
Tucson, AZ 85745

ANIMAL INFORMATION
Assign each student a specific animal and then ask them to research what they eat, if they travel in herds, where they are found, how fast they run, etc.

Students might also like to write letters to the director of a local zoo asking about their experiences with exotic animals. Perhaps a zoologist from a zoo or nearby university can arrange a visit to your classroom.

The National Wildlife Federation has available to teachers many products and books relating to animals around the world. For a free copy of their catalog, call (800) 432-6564.

ZOOLOGICAL AWARDS
During your unit on zoos, award your students with animal crackers or gummy animals for work completed.

You can also use the crackers as manipulatives for counting, grouping, estimating, etc.

ZOO SPECIALISTS
A person who specializes in the study of animals is called a zoologist. However, there are other scientists who specialize in specific species of animals. As your class studies the different types of animals, familiarize students with the person who specializes in that area.

An *Ornithologist* studies birds.
An *Ichthyologist* studies fish.
An *Entomologist* studies insects.
A *Herpetologist* studies reptiles and amphibians.
A *Mammalogist* studies mammals.

DINGO (BINGO)
A dingo is a wild dog found in Australia. Use this play on words to create a fun animal bingo game!

Assign one letter of the alphabet to each child in class. The student must think of two animals that start with his or her assigned letter and write the names on the class board. (Encourage students to use research books to find the names of unusual animals.)

Give each student a copy of a bingo card. Tell the students to choose the names of 24 animals and write them in the squares. Tell them to mark the center square "FREE."

When everyone is ready, call out a name of an animal, using the list on the board. When a student matches a row of animals they shout out the word "DINGO."

Zoo Animal Activities!

UNIQUE ANIMALS

Your students will become more familiar with the unusual animals found in zoos with a simple research assignment. Assign each student an animal name from the list below and ask them to find out the following:

- Is it a mammal, reptile, insect, bird or fish?
- What part of the world is it found?
- What does it look like?
- What does it eat?
- What is its greatest enemy or threat?
- Is it in danger of becoming extinct?
- Name three things that make this animal unusual.
- Draw a picture of your animal.

Aardvark	Komodo Dragon
Ostrich	Sloth
Ferret	Weasel
Albatross	Caribou
Rhinoceros	Otter
Wallaby	Falcon
Salamander	Walrus
Scorpion	Black Mamba
Cheetah	Koala
Chameleon	Bison
Eel	Hyenas
Squid	War Hog
Condor	Orangutan
Wombat	Dingo
Emu	Lynx
Llama	Panda
Tasmanian Devil	Armadillo
Opossum	Platypus

Display the papers on the class board around a world map. String colorful yarn from the map to each paper to show where each animal can be found.

GRASSLANDS OR TROPICAL

More than 40% of Africa is covered in grasslands called savannas, They consist of tall grasses and only a few scattered trees. The climate is usually very warm with a varying rainfall.

The other 60% is made up mostly of large tropical rainforests. A rainforest is made up of large trees and vines that create a canopy for the underlying plants. It is warm and moist throughout the year.

Divide the class into two teams and assign them each to display one of the two African environments on a bulletin board, one with grasslands and the other a tropical forest. Ask students to research the types of animals and plants that live in the two environments. Children can then cut from colored paper grasses, vegetation, trees, animals, birds, reptiles, etc. to display on the appropriate board.

GIRAFFE SPOTS

In this fun classroom display, this giraffe can certainly change its spots!

Laminate a large paper giraffe and display it on the class board. Make sure that you have drawn an ample number of large spots on the giraffe's neck and body. Each week, assign a student to "change" the giraffe's spots! Using dry transfer markers on the lamination, students can write math problems, vocabulary words, improper fractions, etc., on each spot. During free time, students can answer the problems on a separate sheet of paper and turn it in for extra credit. The problems can easily be erased with a soft cloth or tissue.

Children will look forward to the "change of spots" and new problems to solve!

My Animal Report

_____
Student's Name

My animal is a _____
_____
_____

My animal's native habitat is
_____
_____

My animal eats _____
_____

Three interesting facts about my animal:
1. _____
_____
2. _____
_____
3. _____
_____

Here's a drawing of my animal.

My animal can grow to be this size: _____
_____

My animal is: ☐ endangered   ☐ not endangered

My thoughts about this animal! _____
_____
_____
_____

Hippo Paper Bag Puppet

Paste the pattern pieces to a small paper lunch bag.

Lion Paper Bag Puppet

Cut these lion puppet patterns from construction paper. Glue the two pieces to a small, brown paper lunch bag. Sections of pipe cleaners can be added as whiskers.

Have each student make his or her own puppet and role play stories about the animal.

Lion Paper Topper

Cut these lion patterns from colorful paper. Cut the lion's mane along the dotted lines. Curl each strip around a pencil to curl. Display the lion around a "great work paper" poster!

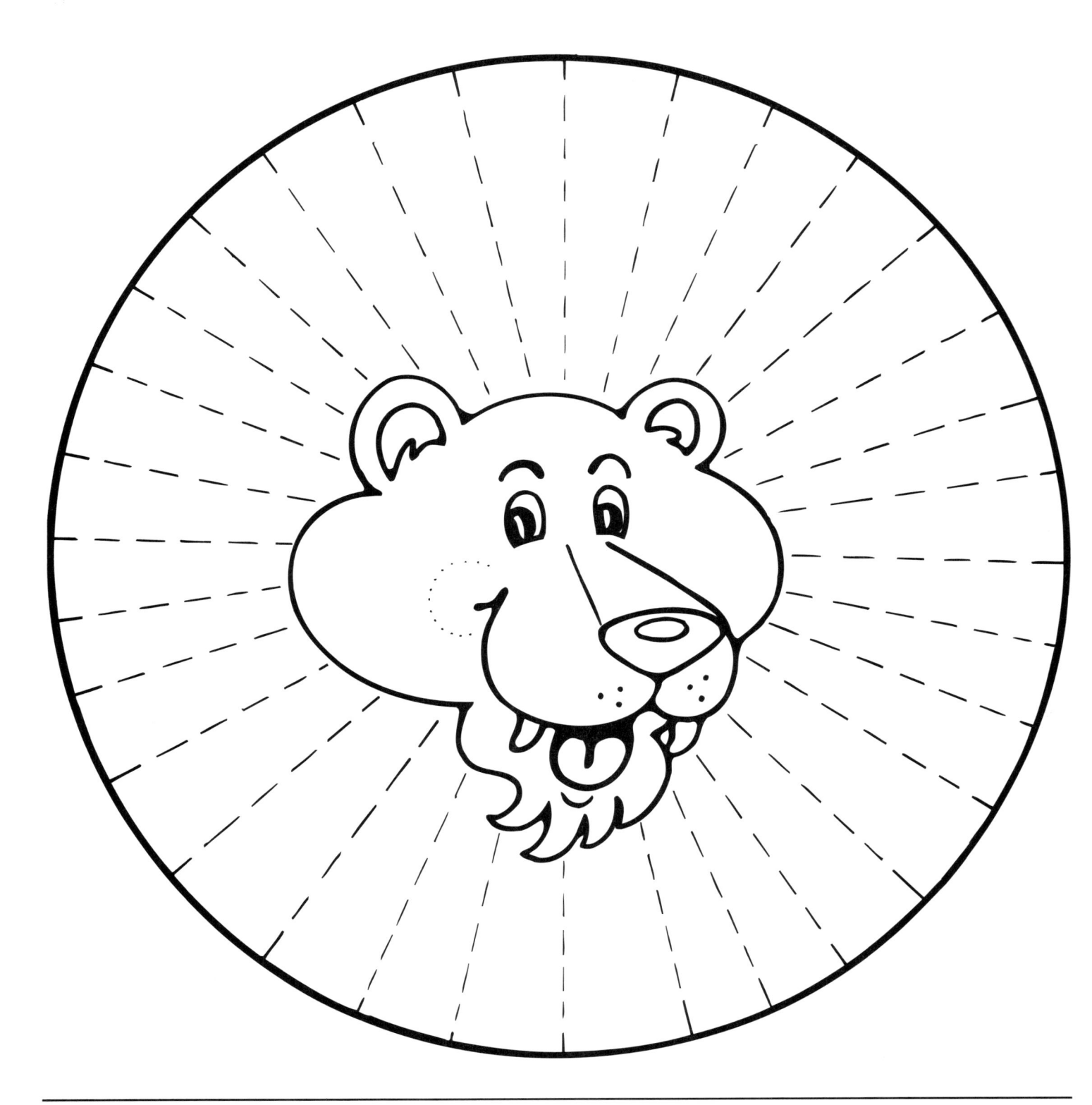

Grrreat Work!

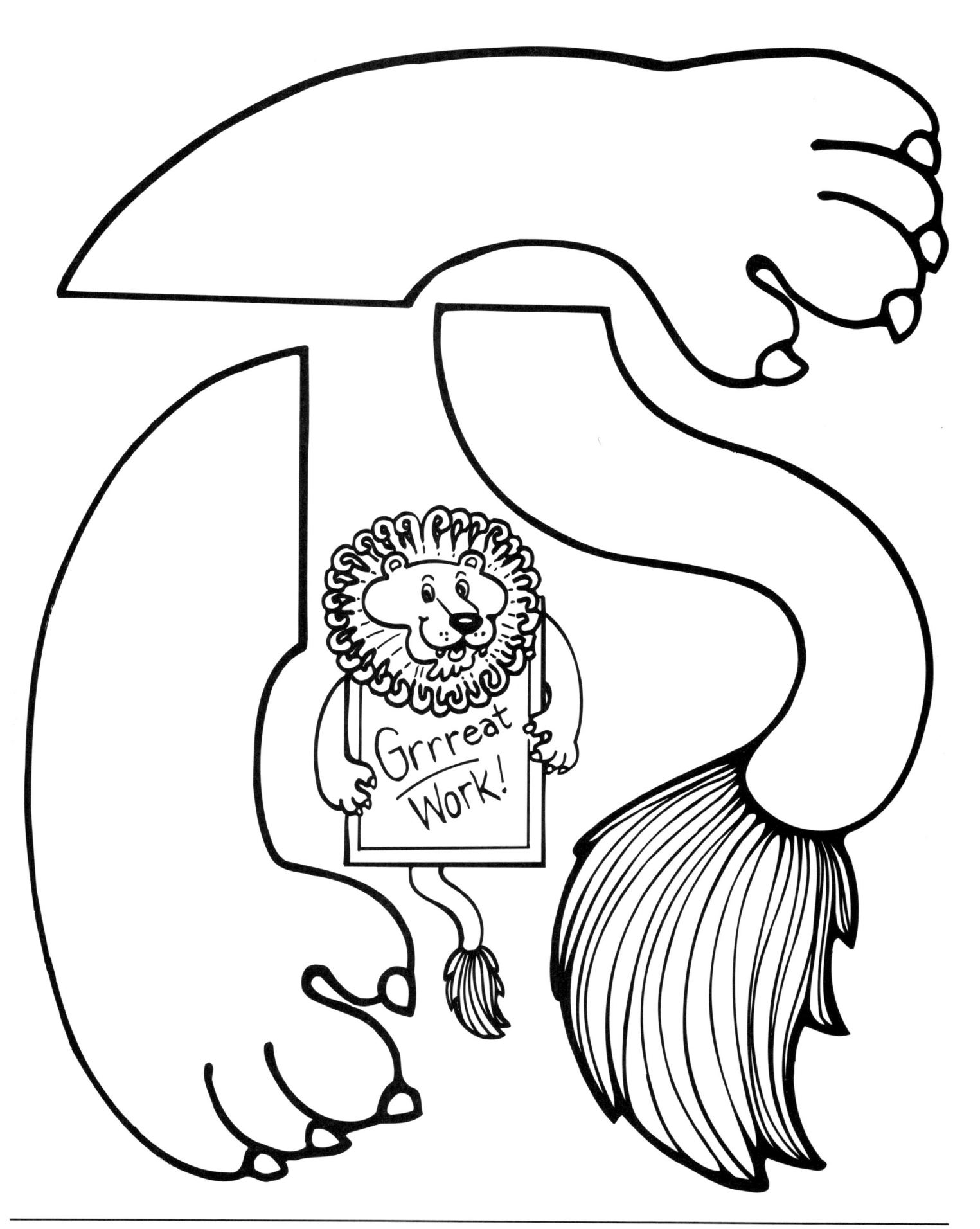

Stand-Up Zoo Animals

Cut these cute zoo animals from folded, colored paper. Use them as name plates or mini booklet covers.

These stand-up animals can also be enlarged and used to designate student groups on the class bulletin board.

Hippo Patterns

Enlarge this hippo and display him on the class bulletin board to illustrate the "huge" success your students are achieving in a various subject areas.

Teacher's Friend Publications, Inc. ©   TF0500 May Idea Book

Bulletin Boards and More!

Bulletin Boards and More!

MAY DAY!
Make this delightful May Day board!

Using the patterns in this chapter, cut several birds from white paper. Display a maypole in the center of the board and add several crepe paper streamers to the top. Arrange the streamers around the board with a bird holding each end.

Students can add their names to the birds.

EARLY BIRD BOARD
Enlarge this cute bird and worm to help display classroom bird watching booklets or reports.

Other bulletin board titles include:
"This is for the Birds!"
"Birds of a Feather..."
"Fly high this spring!"
"The Early Bird Catches the Worm!"

M-O-T-H-E-R
Pay a special tribute to Mom on her day with this bulletin board idea.

Display the letters MOTHER down one side of the class board. Children can write their own special feelings about their moms on strips of paper, making sure each sentence starts with the appropriate letter.

Teacher's Friend Publications, Inc. ©   TF0500 May Idea Book

Bulletin Boards and More!

CLASSMATES IN BLOOM
Your students will "bloom" with pride when they see this flowery board.

Cut large flowers from colored paper and arrange them across the board. Display a snapshot of each child in the center of the flowers or simply write their names in bold marker.

This is a great way to welcome parents during open house!

THE BIG TOP!
Excitement will build when you display this colorful circus circus tent on the class bulletin board.

Cut a large circus tent from striped wallpaper or a brightly colored bed sheet. Fly a circus banner from the top of the tent. Children can design their own circus posters or display drawings of circus animals around the board.

MAKE MOM HAPPY!
Display a large happy face and sad face of mom on either side of a bulletin board. Write the title, "What Makes Mom Happy?" across the top of the board. Children can write their own ideas about what makes mom happy or sad on strips of colored paper. Display these around the board as a Mother's Day reminder.

Teacher's Friend Publications, Inc. ©   TF0500 May Idea Book

Bulletin Boards and More!

EARLY BIRD...
Have each child cut a bird from construction paper and write his or her name on it. Display the birds on the class bulletin board. At the bottom of the board pin green paper grass and dozens of paper worms. As each child completes an assignment, he or she is awarded a worm to place in their bird's mouth.

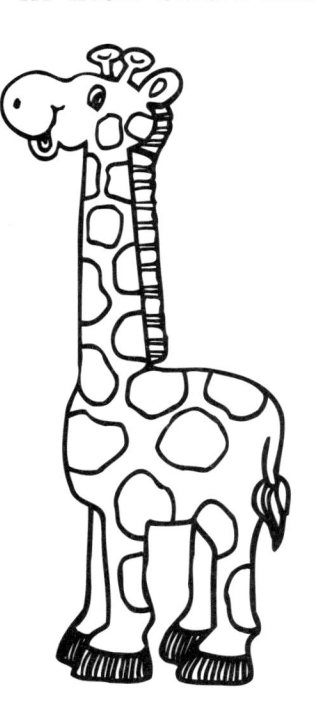

GIRAFFE SPOTS!
Have each student post their own giraffe character on the class board and color its spots as assignments are completed.

You may want to enlarge the giraffe patterns found on page 141 and label each spot with a student's name. Display a sign declaring, "We're Sticking Out Our Necks to Learn As Much As We Can!"

MONKEY TAILS!
Let your students earn their own hanging monkeys when assignments are completed or behavior improved. Tie a clothes line across the classroom and have students hang the earned monkey for everyone to see.

Bird Patterns

egg

Name

bird

worm

Teacher's Friend Publications, Inc. ©　　　　　　　　　TF0500 May Idea Book

Name

Hanging Monkey

Teacher's Friend Publications, Inc. © · 140 · TF0500 May Idea Book

Giraffe Patterns

Have each student make their own giraffe. Students may color the giraffe's spots as they complete assignments or improve behavior.

Elephant Sign

Clown Sign

Answer Key!

ACTIVITY 1

```
Z C V G T Y H N F L Y C A T C H E R E V C
Q W C V G T B G I J K L O P U Y T R E W D
U C H I C K E N N F R T Y H J K I L O O N
A D F G T G B H C E R T Y W R E N F T G H
I D F U R T G C H I C K A D E E V B G H Y
L E R L Y E L L O W H A M M E R R W E C S
V E R L D R E T F G T H B T F O G O O S E
B L U E B I R D D R T G B Y H B W Q X W T
V G H Y U J O R I O L E D R I D C V B G
P E R G D R P T A R M I G A N N E R T Y U
E W Q R C A R D I N A L P H E A S A N T Y
L D R T G F V B N H J U K I O L P M G R T
I T H R U S H E R E R T F G B U N T I N G
C D R E F G T Y H M O C K I N G B I R D Q
A R T Y U I D F V G B N H J K M U Y R E W
N D E R O A D R U N N E R E W Q S D T Y U
G R O U S E G O L D F I N C H W Q E T Y O
X V M E A D O W L A R K F G E F G V B H J
T H R A S H E R E W Q V B N M K J S W R T
```

ACTIVITY 2

```
W T C H J U I K R I N G M A S T E R D C V
X E N C F G V B N H B C F T E L E P H A N T
C N T D G T B A C V G T Y H J U I K M N B G
P T C V B F L I O N S V F T R V B N J H G
O X C I D F L S C I R C U S X C V V G C Y
P V F H B D O F R F B H Y U J N G H Y L U
C O F T G C O T T O N C A N D Y R T H O V
O F T Y H G N C D R T G D S W A C V B W N
R T I G E R S D G R E W D V B N J H G S S
N R B G H T I G H T R O P E V R E F S W
A N I M A L S D F R E T W Q G T Y G V F S
C V G T Y H F D E W D H O R S E S F R T Y
C F A C R O B A T V G T Y H N H T U J I L
C V F T H G R E W A S C V B H Y U I J K L
C D F R E W Q T I C K E T S G T R W Q X D
```

Teacher's Friend Publications, Inc. ©   144   TF0500 May Idea Book